CHINA'S SPLENDORS

CHINA'S SPLENDORS

HUGH LAUTER LEVIN ASSOCIATES, INC.

CHINA'S SPLENDORS

© 2000 HUGH LAUTER LEVIN ASSOCIATES, INC.

Written and Coordinated by: Charles Schoenfeld
Photo Research & Factual Editing: the staff of China Pictorial
Factual Editing: China Travel & Tourism Press
Executive Factual Editor: Gong Weijian, CTTP
Copyediting: Ou Xiaomei and Deborah T. Zindell

Design: Dana Levy, PERPETUA PRESS, Los Angeles

ISBN: 0-88363-158-X

Printed in Hong Kong
Published and distributed in China by China Travel and Tourism Press

http://www.HLLA.com

Contents

Jiayuguan Pass on the Great Wall 7

The Yangtze River 8

The Three Gorges 11

The Lijiang River 12

The Ancient Great Wall 12

Lanzhou, on the Yellow River 19

Cormorant Fishing on the Nanxi River 20

Urho (Devil's Town) 23

Sunrise on Mount Taishan 24

Mount Huashan 27

Wulingyuan Scenic Reserve 28

Pandas in the Wolong Nature Reserve 31

Mount Longhu 32

Yandang Mountains 35

Wuyi Mountain 36

Rice Terraces on Mount Ailao 39

Tea Plantation on Mount Shifeng 40

The Cloud Dispersing Pavilion on Mount Huangshan 43

Sea of Clouds on Mount Huangshan 44

Fengxian Temple, Longmen Grottoes 49

Taklimakan Desert 50

Stone Forest 53

Ashma, in the Stone Forest 54

Seven-Star Cave 57

Grotto No. 45, Mogao Grottoes 58

Grotto No. 285, Mogao Grottoes 61

Dazu Grottoes 62

Yungang Grottoes 65

Buddhist Statues at Yungang Grottoes 66

Jiuzhaigou (Nine-Village Valley) 69

West Lake 70

Lake Taihu 73

Zhaoling Mausoleum 74

Cemetery of Confucius 79

Lake Tianchi (Heavenly Lake) 80

Black Dragon Pool 83

Sunset on Hainan Island 84

Yurts in Axi Pastureland 87

Wild Camels on Barkol Grassland 88

The Grand Canal in Suzhou 91

The Bund 92

Victoria Harbor 95

Harbin Ice Lantern Festival 96

Xiaoling Mausoleum 99

Mausoleum of Dr. Sun Yat-sen 100

Chengde Mountain Resort and Outlying Temples 103

Potala Palace 104

The Forest of Stupas at Shaolin Temple 109

Yellow Crane Tower 110

Leshan Buddha 113

Xuankong (Suspended) Temple 114

Qiyuan Temple on Jiuhua Mountain 117

Diamond Throne Stupa 118

The Three Pagodas of Saintly Worship 121

Flying Dragon White Pagoda 122

Jiayuguan Pass on the Great Wall

GANSU PROVINCE

TODAY, THE JIAYUGUAN PASS is the best preserved of all the passes on the Great Wall. In ancient times, it was one of the most strategically valuable points on the entire length of the wall. Sandwiched between the Qilian Mountains to the south and the Mazong (Horse's Mane) Mountains to the north, the fortress known as *Cheng Lou* guarded the only viable pass between mainland China and the Qingzang Plateau of China and central Asia. Planted on a flat stone desert between the two mountain ranges, the tall and forbidding fort is still an awe-inspiring sight. To the north of the fort, segments of the Great Wall itself remain intact.

Jiayuguan Fort was built in the Ming Dynasty, in the year 1372. Its outer wall is 10 meters high and over 700 meters in length. It is 5 meters thick at the bottom, supported by a lower wall made of rammed earth, and 2 meters thick at the top. Along the top are crenellations, which give the fort an imposing silhouette in the sunset. Inside the outer wall's single gate is an inner wall of rammed earth, equipped with watchtowers and a rampart where invading armies could be trapped and defeated. Two gates on the inner wall give access to sloping pathways by which horse-mounted archers could

ascend to patrol the tops of the walls. During the later years of the Ming Dynasty, Jiayuguan's garrison consisted of about one thousand soldiers. A stele outside the outer gate reads: "Greatest Barrier Under Heaven."

A local folk legend tells that one of the masons who built the fort, named Yi Kaizhan, was so skilled that when he calculated the number of bricks the project would require, he came within one brick of the exact answer. The "extra" brick still sits displayed on an upper ledge.

In the minds of many Chinese, the city of Jiayuguan retains its historical reputation as a desolate frontier, the last bastion of civilization before embarking into an uncertain and barbaric wilderness. During the Ming Dynasty, Jiayuguan was the last Chinese outpost on the Silk Road, the westernmost point of "civilization." Anyone leaving westward through this gate knew that they were leaving behind everything they called home—a fact poignantly reinforced by the bleakness of the landscape. A ninth-century poet wrote of a leave-taking at Jiayuguan: "One more cup of wine for our remaining happiness. There will be chilling parting dreams tonight."

The Yangtze River

THE YANGTZE RIVER (also called Changjiang, "long river"), is more than 6,300 kilometers long. It is the longest river in China and the third longest in the world, after the Amazon and the Nile.

Flowing from the chilly heights of the Qinghai–Tibet Plateau down to the East China Sea, it passes through a total of eight provinces, two municipalities, and one autonomous region: Qinghai, Tibet, Yunnan, Sichuan, Hubei, Hunan, Jiangxi, Anhui, Jiangsu, Chongqing, and Shanghai. If you could walk its length—not a journey for any but the boldest and hardiest—you would experience much of the remarkably varied scenery of central and southern China. From the high plateau of Qinghai, the river, here called the Golden Sands, takes a huge bend by the town of Shigu in Yunnan Province, only to turn south again before settling on an eastward course. It shortly encounters Tiger Leap Gorge, where it is forced to squeeze between snow-capped mountains. In the big bend region, the many twists of the river have carved out swathes of excellent fertile land that is densely cultivated.

The tourist area of the Yangtze is concentrated in three provinces–Sichuan, Hubei, and Hunan. The subtropical climate here makes for muggy summers and mild winters. The region's attractions include enchanting mountain-and-water scenery, sites of historic significance, ancient ruins, hot springs in which to bathe, and prosperous, charming small towns.

The greatest natural highlight along the river is Sanxia, the famous Three Gorges, one of the world's great canyons. Downriver of the Three Gorges there are other sights. The Chibi Cliffs and the Three Midstream Rocky Cliffs were both made famous by poets: Su Shi of the Song Dynasty, and Li Bai of the Tang, respectively. Stone Bell Hill is said to ring like a giant bell as the wind blows through its many caverns. And Xiaogu (Small Solitary) Hill, with temples and pavilions decorated in pink and green, resembles a giant lotus flower sitting on the water.

Hubei Province has preserved many ancient sites, and offers tours surveying the history of the Three Kingdoms, and the ancient conflicts between the local states of Wei, Shu, and Wu. Sichuan Province boasts a massive irrigation system–Dujiangyan Weir–more than two thousand years old, as well as the world famous Great Buddha at Leshan, and the stone sculptures at Dazu, splendid examples of the later period of Chinese grotto art.

The Three Gorges

CHONGQING MUNICIPALITY & HUBEI PROVINCE

A BOAT CRUISE DOWN the Changjiang (Yangtze) River is a worthwhile experience because of the deservedly famous Three Gorges alone. Qutang, Wuxia, and Xiling Gorges–known collectively as Sanxia–lie along a 193-kilometer stretch of river that extends from White Emperor City of Fengjie County, in Chongqing Municipality, eastward to the Nanjin Pass of Yichang City, in Hubei Province. Sheer cliffs and steep mountains rise up into the clouds on either side of the river, creating a magnificent sight. And the Yangtze flows strong and turbulent through Sanxia, swelling with water from its tributaries in Sichuan Province.

Qutang Gorge, which, at eight kilometers in length, is the shortest of the three, is best known for the majesty of its sheer cliff faces, which tower above the river on both sides, almost blocking the sun and the sky from view. At Kuimen Gate, the precipices measure less than 100 meters apart.

Wuxia Gorge offers a more subdued charm, seen most conspicuously in the serene beauty of the Wushan's famous Twelve Peaks, between which the river twists and turns. Of these, Goddess Peak is the most arresting and probably the best known. The "Goddess" is named for its nymph-like shape, and is at its most beautiful in the morning and evening, when enshrouded by mists.

Xiling Gorge is the longest, at 76 kilometers, and the favorite of most sightseers. It has been said that Xiling "tops the world for its mountains and waters." The currents in this area flow rapidly, and the waters are dotted with perilous shoals–shallow spots that present a hazard to navigation. And some of the peaks and cliffs–with their dizzying height and surreal shapes–defy the imagination. The cliffs are peppered with overhanging rocks, and mountain springs spill down the cliff faces like glistening ribbons.

There are various historical relics to be found in the area around the Three Gorges, including White Emperor City, the Temple of Zhangfei, Gaotang Pass, the home village of Zhaojun, and the birthplace of Qu Yuan.

The Changjiang's Three Gorges have even inspired imitators; other scenic areas have been named for them, including the "Lesser Three Gorges" on the Daning River, and yet another three gorges on the Jialing River. However, despite the undeniable beauty of these other sites, there is no substitute and no competition for the original Three Gorges–for Sanxia.

The Lijiang River (Opposite)

IT IS OFTEN SAID THAT THE SCENERY of Guilin—the mountains, waters, and caves seen on the 83-kilometer stretch of river between Guilin and Yangshuo in south China—is the most beautiful scenery found anywhere under Heaven. In some places soft and verdant, in other places majestic and almost surreal, Guilin's scenery has long delighted tourists and nature lovers.

The water of the Lijiang River is astonishingly clear in places. As was once said, "The water . . . is so clear that despite the depth of the river one can see to the bottom, the pebbles on it, the veins on the pebbles, the glistening of the sand and the traces left on the sand by crawling insects . . ." At other times, the water takes on lush, vibrant colors: blues and greens, possibly reflections of the sky and the surrounding trees.

Traveling down the river, one will see villages of white-walled farmhouses, surrounded by gardens of rice, fruit, and vegetables, with fishing boats on the river. The scenery also includes *karst* formations—tall, jagged peaks of limestone, sometimes covered with vegetation. The whole of this region was once seabed. Exposed to the air, it weathered in the warm, humid climate, eroded by rain and feathered with vegetation. And on the banks of the river, there are the beautiful osmanthus trees. With their red, golden, and silver flowers, the osmanthus lend not only rich colors, but also a delightful sweet scent to the Guilin region.

The Ancient Great Wall (Overleaf)

THE CREDIT FOR THE CONCEPTION and construction of the Great Wall is usually given to the first emperor of the Qin Dynasty, Qin Shi Huang, more than to any other single person. It was he who first unified the many warring Chinese states, and ordered that a force of 300,000 soldiers and conscripted citizens build a protective wall more than 10,000 *li* in length (a *li* is equal to half a kilometer) around the borders of his empire. These workers, though—as fatally arduous as their task often was—did not have to start from scratch. Wall-building had been a common practice for centuries by the time their work got underway.

As early as the Spring and Autumn Period (770–476 B.C.), China consisted of seven small states in the vicinity of the Huanghe (Yellow) and Changjiang (Yangtze) rivers. The princes who ruled these states were constantly at war with one another and with nomadic tribes from outside their borders. They fortified their domains first by building isolated beacon towers and guard houses, and then went on to connect these structures with walls, usually made of locally available materials such as rocks and rammed earth.

Pictured here are the ruins of the wall of the State of Qi, in Shandong Province on China's east coast. Construction of the Great Wall of Qi had already begun in the fifth century B.C. Its main purpose was to protect against invasions from its southern neighbor, the State of Chu. The Qi wall stretched one thousand *li* from modern Pingyin County in the west to the sea in the east. Ruins of this wall still exist in and around the cities of Laiwu and Tai'an. Depending on how well they have weathered the passage of time, these wall fragments range from one to four meters in height, and four to five meters in thickness.

The Great Wall did more than keeping out military invasions. It also kept in the essence of Chinese-ness, which distinguished China from the "barbarian" nations outside the wall. A Scottish doctor visiting Beijing in the eighteenth century remarked of the Great Wall's construction: "I am of the opinion that no nation in the world was able for such an undertaking, except the Chinese. For, though some other kingdom might have furnished a sufficient number of workmen . . . none but the ingenious, sober, and parsimonious Chinese could have preserved order amidst such labor."

Lanzhou, on the Yellow River

HE HUANGHE (YELLOW RIVER) flows through Gansu Province. Originating on the Qinghai–Tibet Plateau and emptying into the Bohai Sea, the Huanghe is not only the second longest river in China, it's also the muddiest in the world. As the Huanghe flows through the Loess Plateau, it takes away large quantities of fine-grained loess soil, greatly increasing its own silt content and causing serious soil erosion on the plateau.

The city of Lanzhou, located near the geographic center of China, is the capital of Gansu Province. The modern city, home to more than two million people, is a hub for regional communications and transportation. Its major industries are machine production and petro-chemicals.

Lanzhou has a long history. The city has been important for thousands of years because of its position in the Hexi Corridor, or Corridor West of the Yellow River, where Chinese civilization began. About three thousand years ago, during the Zhou Dynasty, agriculture began to take shape in the basins of the Jin and Wei rivers, marking the beginning of the great Yellow River basin civiliza-tion. Lanzhou first came to prosperity as a stop on the trade route known as the Silk Road, which ran west from Xi'an all the way to the Roman Empire. It was to protect Lanzhou that the Han Dynasty extended the Great Wall as far as Yumen, in the far northwest of what is now Gansu Province.

Lanzhou also has its share of religious sites, such as Bingling Temple, with its cave shrines and stone statues, as well as a 27-meter-high Buddha. Lanzhou became capital of a succession of tribal states following the decline of the Han. During these dangerous times, people turned to various faiths to bring hope and meaning to their lives. Taoism and Buddhism developed and flourished, and shrines were built in temples, caves, and on cliffs. Nearby Dunhuang, another city in Gansu Province, is also an important center for Buddhist study and art.

Outside Lanzhou's borders, much of the land in Gansu Province is dedicated to grain farming and the raising of livestock. Thanks to the fertile climate, one can also find vegetables, peaches, and honeydew melons growing along the banks of the Huanghe River.

Cormorant Fishing on the Nanxi River

THE NANXI RIVER MEANDERS through the southern part of Zhejiang Province in a large area of over 500 square miles, making about thirty major bends and, in the dry season, fertilizing more than double the number of beaches that are cultivable as it leaves deposits of mineral-rich soil from the river in flood. As it passes through Yongjia County, the river features some eight hundred scenic spots along its length, both natural and artificially created. These include Daruoyan, the twelfth holy spot of the Taoist faith, as well as Taogong Cave, Wengchang Pavilion, Chishui Well, and Baichang Waterfall.

In this photo of the scenic area near Shizi (Lion) Rock, fishermen on the Nanxi River, in their pencil-thin crafts, use trained cormorants to catch fish. This traditional technique of fishing has been practiced in various parts of east Asia for the last thirteen hundred years, passed down from generation to generation. It is a common sight not only on the Nanxi River, but also on the Lijiang, and in Japan.

Upon command, one of the several birds waiting patiently on the front of the craft plunges into the still waters, provoking a spread of ripples on the surface. Time passes—perhaps whole min-utes—as the fisherman waits patiently. Finally, the bird returns to the surface with a fish thrashing in its beak. The fisherman claims the fish, drops it into a large wicker basket at the rear of the boat, and sends the next bird into the water.

In addition to their training, the cormorants are tied to the boat by strings attached to their legs; and the leashes around their necks have rings, or simple twine knots, narrow enough to prevent them from swallowing the fish they catch, but not tight enough to asphyxiate them. From time to time, the fisherman removes the leash and rewards the bird with a fish.

Cormorants can grow to nearly a meter in length. They have long, flexible necks; large, hooked bills; thick, glossy black plumage; webbed feet, and stiff tails. They are related to pelicans, and make their nests on the seacoasts of the world's temperate and tropical regions. The great cormorant and the Japanese cormorant are the two species used for fishing in Asia. A common myth has it that they keep their wings extended for balance because their high centers of gravity make them less adept at walking than at flying and swimming. The truth is simply that they need to dry their wings after swimming.

Urho (Devil's Town)

I N TERMS OF CLIMATE AND TERRAIN, the Xinjiang Uygur Autonomous Region is a land of extremes. Primarily a harsh land-scape of deserts and mountains, Xinjiang is home to the driest, hottest, and coldest settings in China, as well as the country's longest inland river, its lowest point, and its broadest desert. It is a local saying that in Xinjiang, one can find different weather conditions within an area of a hundred square miles, and four seasons simultaneously in the same valley. The region consists of two giant basins—the Jungar Basin in the north, and the Tarim Basin in the south—separated by the Tianshan (Heavenly) Mountain range.

The Jungar Basin is made up of sandstone, mudstone, and clay dating from the Late Permian through the Late Cretaceous periods. The discovery of dinosaur fossils has brought the world's attention to Jungar. But the land is noteworthy even indepen-dent of any bones it may contain. Jungar is home to one of the more exotic landscapes in China—comparable in shape to Yunnan's famous Stone Forest, but altogether different in mood. Whereas the Stone Forest is majestic and tranqil like a forest of trees, made festive by its friendly inhabitants, Urho (the "Wind City," also known as the "City of Devils") offers a more eerie, even delightfully sinister atmosphere.

Imagine yourself walking across this dry, stone landscape. The sky seems unusually vast overhead, meeting the ground at a flat edge that stretches all the way around you. The ground is uneven, wavy, as if it were a stone blanket thrown over a field of lumpy objects. Some of the lumps are tall enough to be called peaks, and some of these are thick enough to resemble buildings. Some of the buildings are lumped together to form what look like castles, and in fact, there is a U-shaped "city wall" of stone enclosing the whole area. And just as it occurs to you to wonder what kind of creature could control the winds to sculpt for itself a stone castle, you hear the *sound* of the Wind City. It starts as a low, keening wail, becomes too faint to hear, and then comes at you with renewed intensity, a plaintive howl that builds to a crescendo of ghost-like screams as a strong wind whips across the plain. When the wind and the sound die together, you realize the truth—the wind has been playing the landscape like a bottle-organ.

Sunrise on Mount Taishan

Mount Taishan, or simply Mount Tai, is the foremost of China's Five Sacred Mountains, and has held great religious significance for more than three thousand years. Located in Tai'an City near the center of Shandong Province, Taishan is also known as the Eastern Mountain; the other four sacred mountains are Hengshan, the Southern Mountain, in Hunan Province; Huashan, the Western Mountain, in Shaanxi Province; the other Mount Hengshan—yes, there are two different sacred mountains both named "Hengshan"—the Northern Mountain, in Shanxi Province; and Songshan, the Central Mountain, in Henan Province.

Taishan's status as the most important of the five mountains derives in part from its placement in the east, the cardinal direction that, according to the doctrine of five elements, signifies birth and spring. For three thousand years, emperors of each dynasty came to Taishan to worship, offering sacrifices to Heaven and Earth.

Evidence of human activity on Taishan dates back 400,000 years, to Yiyuan Man of the Paleolithic period. The mountain had attained cultural significance by the Neolithic period, with the Dawenkou people to the north and the Longshan to the south. But Taishan is best known as a center of the Taoist and Buddhist faiths, with 22 temples, 97 ruins, 819 stone tablets, and over 1,000 stone inscriptions. The Buddhist Divine Rock Temple—dating from 350 B.C.–is considered one of China's four temple wonders, while several hundred thousand Taoist worshippers visited the Azure Cloud Temple each year during the Ming Dynasty (1368–1644). Guo Moruo, a modern Chinese scholar, called Taishan "a partial miniature of Chinese culture."

Taishan is also renowned for its scenic beauty, and the profusion of temples and other man-made artifacts have been designed to exist in harmony with that natural landscape. The remarkable artistry with which that was accomplished is no small part of what makes Taishan such a treasure. Nine kilometers of stone steps lead from the Temple of Taishan at the base of the mountain, past well-known spots such as Zhongtianmen (Halfway to Heaven Gate) , Sutra Stone Valley, Sun-Observing Peak, and Black Dragon Pool.

The summit, Jade Emperor's Peak, towers 1,545 meters above sea level, flanked by Guanri Pavilion to the east and Wanghe Pavilion to the west. The Tang Dynasty poet Du Fu described his experience of the mountain: "Climbing to the summit, the surrounding hills seem to become mole hills." Upon reaching the top, he is alleged to have said, "The world is small."

Mount Huashan

O F THE FIVE SACRED MOUNTAINS in China that are holy to members of the Taoist faith, Mount Taishan is considered the most important, partly due to its placement in the east. However, Mount Huashan, the Western Mountain, is both the tallest and the most scenically impressive of the five. The Chinese call it by the popular name "Number One Steepest Mountain Under Heaven." There is only one negotiable route to the top, along narrow steps cut into the cliffs, and it is so perilous that iron rails have been installed for the safety of climbers. The path traverses such dizzying stretches of cliff as the "Thousand-Foot Precipice," "Hundred-Foot Gorge," "Somersault Cliff," "Ear-Touching Cliff," "Up the Heaven's Ladder," and "Blue Dragon Ridge."

Mount Huashan is located in the south of Huayin County, Shaanxi Province, a mere 120 kilometers east of the ancient imperial capital city of Xi'an. Huashan overlooks the Huanghe (Yellow) River and the Weihe River to the north, and backs up onto the Qinling mountain range to the south.

With its steep peaks and cliffs reaching sharply into the sky, the mountain has been said to resemble a flower, and thus its name is derived from the Chinese word *hua*, meaning "flower." Mount Huashan has five major peaks. Together, these look like the five fingers of a hand reaching skyward, and the sight has been nicknamed "Huashan God's Hand." The southern peak, Luoyan (Peak of the Wild Geese), is the tallest at 2,160 meters above sea level, and it has at the top a large pond of crystal-clear water. Of the other four major peaks, the taller two are the eastern Peak of the Rising Sun and the western Lotus Flower peak, and the smaller two are the central Yunu (Jade Maiden) peak and the northern Yuntai (Cloud Terrace) peak.

Because of Huashan's religious significance, various temples and monasteries have been built there throughout the centuries. Both for aesthetic and practical, architectural reasons, these buildings have been designed in accordance with the existing variations in the terrain. Many emperors, including Gaozu, Taizhong, and princess Jinxian (all of the Tang Dynasty), came to Huashan to worship. Chen Tuan, a founder of the Taoist faith, lived there for nearly forty years.

Wulingyuan Scenic Reserve

HUNAN PROVINCE

I N A COUNTRY WHERE seemingly every scenic mountain has been adopted as a holy site by one religion or another, and nearly every peak has a temple, monastery, pagoda, or pavilion built near its summit, it is particularly impressive to find a scenic area that has been recognized as one of China's essential sights not for its historical significance, but simply for its natural resources. Wulingyuan Scenic Reserve is just such a locale. Although a Han Dynasty (206 B.C.– A.D. 220) lord lived there in seclusion and the Tang Dynasty writer Liu Zhongyuan made reference to the area's beauty, most ancients simply considered the place wild and inaccessibly remote. Today, it has been designated a World Heritage site by UNESCO, for its lovely scenery and its concentration of rare plant and animal species.

Wulingyuan covers an area of nearly 400 square kilometers in the northwest of Hunan Province. Within its borders are 550 tree species–twice the number found in all of Europe–and endangered animals such as giant salamanders and clouded leopards. Wulingyuan's major sightseeing spots are Zhangjiajie State Forest Park (also known as Qingyan, or Green Rock, Mountain), Suoxi Valley, and Mount Tianzi.

On Qingyan Mountain, the main attraction is the concentration of quartzite peaks and pillars, many of them over 200 meters tall. In the slanted rays of the sun and a thin mist, these pinnacles of pale stone, tufted with vegetation, look like precious trinkets from a giant's treasure chest. A variety of wild flowers, mountain streams, and native birds add color to this wonderland.

Suoxi Valley is a natural zoological garden. One can take a river cruise down the gorges between craggy peaks, and admire the spectacular waterfalls and rock formations. Many of Wulingyuan's most exotic animals call this valley home as well. One of the best-known sights is Huanglong Dong (Yellow Dragon Cave), a series of limestone caverns traversed by an underground river.

The Mount Tianzi scenic zone, pictured here, is an area of 93 square kilometers, featuring the highest and most majestic peak in Wulingyuan. Kunlun, the summit of Mount Tianzi, rises to an altitude of 1,262 meters above sea level. The site offers eighty-four natural viewing platforms overlooking misty sylvan valleys, as well as waterfalls, karst caves, and natural stone bridges such as "Immortals' Bridge," across the tops of deep canyons. Local legends say that an ancient Tujia chieftain named Xiang launched a rebellion against imperial forces on this peak, and, upon his defeat, committed suicide by leaping into a valley of stone pinnacles.

Pandas in the Wolong Nature Reserve

Sichuan Province

THE CHINESE GOVERNMENT created the first giant panda reserve in 1963. Of the ten panda reserves now in existence, the Wolong (Reclining Dragon) Nature Reserve in the Qionglai Mountain is the largest, with a total of 785 square miles of land area. It is located near the center of the giant pandas' current range, at 6,500 feet above sea level.

In 1980, the World Wildlife Fund and the Chinese government began a joint effort to study the giant pandas in the Wolong Reserve, with the intention of learning how to help the giant pandas survive as a species. Much of what is now known about the giant pandas was learned from these studies. Researchers tagged the pandas with radio monitoring collars, learned to differentiate the footprints of individual pandas in the snow, and spent many hours tracking the pandas through the wilderness, examining their droppings, and learning their individual eating and sleeping habits, while doing their best not to interfere with those habits.

They also studied extensively the nutritional value and other properties of bamboo, which is the primary component of the giant pandas' diet. Pandas eat bamboo leaves, shoots, and stems, as much as forty-five pounds per day. There are hundreds of species of bamboo, each with different nutritional contents, and pandas need a variety. It takes bamboo about a year to regenerate from seed, and up to ten years before it can support a panda population. The limited supply of bamboo within the pandas' range therefore creates problems for the species' survival.

The Wolong Reserve is currently being used to take sick pandas out of the forest, nurse them back to health, and return them to the forest again. Studies in artificial breeding are also being done, in the hope of increasing the pandas' numbers by releasing newly bred cubs into the wild.

An adult giant panda is typically between 5.25 and 6 feet long, weighing between 80 and 125 kg (176 to 276 pounds). They are similar in shape to bears, although they also share many physical characteristics with raccoons. The fur is made up of a coarse outer layer with black and white markings, and a dense, wooly undercoat. The outer fur has an oily coating that protects the panda from the cool, damp climate. The panda has sharp claws that make it easy to climb trees—and powerful molars and a tough digestive tract with which to digest bamboo stalks. Pandas are solitary animals, preferring not to share the company of other pandas. They move slowly and purposefully, but can move at a slow trot when trying to escape danger.

Mount Longhu

THE PROVINCE OF JIANGXI, situated between the Yangtze River to the north and a mountainous border with Guangdong and Hunan provinces to the south, has spent much of its history as a politically insignificant, and therefore scenically unspoiled, backwater. Populated only lightly for thousands of years, Jiangxi did not see its first massive influx of settlers until the Han Dynasty. Both then and during the subsequent Six Dynasties period, migrants fleeing from the north to escape foreign invaders settled on the plains around Lake Poyang, China's largest freshwater lake. Today, two of Jiangxi's greatest attractions are the revolutionary memorial spots—it has the most of any province in the country—and the town of Jingdezhen, the main producer of porcelain in China.

Besides Lake Poyang, the main scenic attractions in Jiangxi Province include Lushan Mountain in the north and the Jinggang mountain range in the south. Once covered with temples, Lushan has more recently been recognized by travellers—including such notables as Chiang Kai-shek and Harry Truman—as an ideal summer resort. Jinggangshan is known as the "Cradle of the Chinese Revolution." The troops of Mao Zedong, Zhu De, and Peng Dehuai met here in 1927.

Meanwhile, in Xixian County in the northeast of Jiangxi, 20 kilometers south of the copper-mining town of Yingtan, lies another state-protected scenic mountain. The mountain retreat known as Longhushan (Dragon and Tiger Mountain), though less significant than the Five Holy Mountains, is recognized as sacred by the Taoist faith. According to legend, the founder of Taoism, Zhang Ling, once took up residence on this mountain. Also on Mount Longhu, Zhang Daoling became the first Taoist pope of China.

The name "Dragon and Tiger" derives from the appearance of the mountain's two main peaks, which seem to stand face to face, like a dragon and a tiger staring each other down. Altogether, the mountain has ninety-nine peaks, with sixty-six identified scenic spots. The Southern Praying Mantis style of *kung fu* was developed in the mountain's bamboo forest. With its vegetation-covered rocky peaks and slopes reflected in the Shangqing River, and its sprinkling of colorful flowers, this beautiful mountain resembles a miniature version of the famous Three Gorges in places.

Yandang Mountains

Zhejiang Province is the third smallest of China's twenty-eight provinces and autonomous regions, after Taiwan and Ningxia, but is also one of the wealthiest. It is replete with areas of scenic splendor, including Hangzhou's exquisite West Lake, and Mount Putuo, one of the four mountains most sacred to Chinese Buddhists—not to be confused with the Five Sacred Mountains of the Taoist faith. In the north, Zhejiang's climate is hot in the summer and cold in the winter; the land is fertile and the waterways highly travelled. The south is less densely populated, and more mountainous, with a more tropical climate.

The southeastern city of Wenzhou, in particular, is known for its superb scenery, particularly Jiangxinyu Island and North Yandang Mountain. *Wenzhou* means "mild prefecture," a reference to the area's very pleasant subtropical monsoonal climate, which remains warm in the winter and cool in the summer. It is a coastal city with strong fishing and transportation industries.

The Yandang (meaning, "Wild Goose and Reed Marsh") Mountains are divided into South Yandang Mountain and North Yandang Mountain. The Northern Yandang Mountain Scenic Area is located in Leqing County, about three hours' travel, or about 80 kilometers, to the northeast of Wenzhou. It is sometimes said to be the Number One Mountain in southeastern China for beautiful scenery. Within a scenic area that covers about 400 square kilometers can be seen some stunning peaks; majestic cliffs; elegant, tranquil streams and pools; deep, quiet valleys and canyons; rocks of strange and interesting shapes; and tall waterfalls like shimmering ribbons of silk. There have also been Buddhist shrines, temples, and monasteries built on the verdant slopes of the mountain. Among the roughly 380 scenic spots that have been named on the North Yandang Mountain, the four best-known and most splendid are Lingfeng and Lingyan Peaks, and the Longqiu (Great and Small Dragon) Cataracts.

Wuyi Mountain

FUJIAN PROVINCE

Wuyi MOUNTAIN, an area whose scenic complexity is belied by the simple name "mountain," has long enjoyed a reputation for surpassing the whole of southeast China in beauty.

Located in the city of Wuyishan, in the northwestern part of Fujian Province, Wuyi Mountain has thirty-six peaks of black volcanic rock, several taller than 1,500 meters. Large fault structures, water erosion, and weathering, combined with the region's volcanic activity, have contributed to the formation of sheer cliffs of red sandstone, dome-shaped precipices, cave systems, and winding streams. The gorges of the aptly-named Jiuqu (Nine Bends) Stream, serene and covered with vegetation, offer some especially dramatic scenery.

Wuyi's splendors have been protected since as far back as the eighth century, when the emperor decreed that its natural landscape should remain untouched. In 1979, the State Council of China designated Wuyi Mountain and its surrounding 570 square kilometers as the Mount Wuyi Nature Reserve, continuing the tradition of protection. Mount Wuyi was inscribed on UNESCO's list of World Heritage sites in 1999.

In addition to its scenic beauty, Wuyi Mountain has its share of archaeological and cultural significance. Evidence of human activity in the area dates back as far as the twenty-first century B.C. Cave dwellings, rock inscriptions, and pottery have all been discovered. An ancient city of the Min Yue people dates back more than 2,300 years; and in the first century B.C., the Han Dynasty rulers built a large capital city at nearby Chengcun. More recent artifacts of comparable importance include the temples and monasteries from the eleventh century A.D., many of them now in ruins, where Neo-Confucianism first developed.

Yet another of Mount Wuyi's treasures is the great variety of vegetation and wildlife that flourishes there. The variations in plant life depend mostly on the elevation, but the forests of broad-leaved evergreens are probably the most ecologically important, as they include some of the world's largest tracts of humid subtropical forest. The world-famous tea *Dahongpao* also grows here. Some five thousand species of wildlife have also been catalogued on and around Mount Wuyi, including such rare specimens as the miniature monkey and the hummingbird, as well as migratory birds, more than one hundred of which are protected by Chinese agreements with Japan and Australia.

Rice Terraces on Mount Ailao

YUNNAN PROVINCE

THE AILAO MOUNTAIN RANGE is in Yunnan Province, in the southwestern part of China. In this photo, we can see farmers tending their rice terraces. Rice is the dominant crop in the southern part of China, and the farmers have developed this system of flooded hillside terraces to help control the irrigation of their rice, and thereby, the balance of nutrients in the soil.

Rice is the main dietary staple of half the world's population, and the world produces 520 million tons of rice each year. China has devoted more than ninety percent of its arable land to raising crops. This is a necessity, given the country's tremendous population density; China must feed twenty-three percent of the world's population using only seven percent of the world's farmland. Fortunately, in southern China the warm climate allows farmers to have two or even three harvests each year, yielding as much as six tons of rice per hectare of land.

Archaeologists believe that rice cultivation began in China roughly 11,500 years ago, along the middle part of the Yangtze River. Rice grains, grain impressions, and plant remains have been found to support this conclusion in samples of ancient pottery excavated from more than one hundred sites throughout Hubei and Hunan provinces. These dates show that rice cultivation predated both millet farming in China, which began about 7,500 years ago, and the world's oldest evidence of barley farming, which dates from 10,000 years ago in Israel.

The successful cultivation of rice paddies requires endless hard work. The system of canals, terraces, and reservoirs must be carefully designed and painstakingly maintained. The labor that goes into planting, harvesting, and threshing the rice is backbreaking. First, seedlings are obtained by sowing rice into specially prepared seedbeds. After several weeks the seedlings are transplanted to a flooded field or terrace where they are left to grow in two to eight inches of water for several months. Two to three weeks before harvest, the paddy is drained. The rice stalks are cut and tied into bundles and allowed to dry before threshing. It has been estimated that a farmer must grow six hundred kilos of rice per year just to feed and clothe himself, and a farmer with dependents must obviously do considerably more.

Tea Plantation on Mount Shifeng

IN THE CITY OF HANGZHOU, Zhejiang Province, a short distance to the west of the splendid West Lake lies the village of Longjing. Here, on the slopes of Shifeng (Lion Peak) Mountain, terraced tea plantations rise on all sides behind the houses. This locale is famous as the birthplace, and continued center of production, of Longjing (Dragon Well) tea, the finest green tea in China.

There is some debate over whether the brewing of tea originated in China's southwest or came to China from India, but in either case, people have been drinking tea for centuries. China has had tea plants for nearly six thousand years, and they have been cultivated for two millennia. Tea, along with porcelain and silk, has long been one of China's most significant exports.

Dragon Well tea is a green tea, the least processed of all varieties of tea. These leaves produce a pure and clear beverage with a light, refreshing fragrance. Green tea is prepared with hot, but *not boiling* water—it turns bitter if brewed too hot. The Chinese also say that the second infusion brewed from green tea leaves produces the best flavor.

According to the Tang Dynasty tea expert Lu Yu, the first tea on Mount Shifeng was grown in Tianzhu and Lingying temples. It was named "Dragon Well" tea in the Song Dynasty, after the Longjing Spring near the foot of the village. The Song Dynasty writer Su Dongpo carved three characters meaning "Old Dragon Well" near the foot of the mountain, as a tribute to the tea. The gardens gained fame in the Ming and Qing dynasties, among common folk in addition to the monks of the temples. The Qing emperor Qianlong visited the area four times, and designated the eighteen tea trees in front of Hugong Temple "royal tea."

The conditions on Mount Shifeng are uniquely suited to tea-growing. The land is low in acidity and rich in minerals. The mountain slopes shield the plants from hot southern breezes and cold northern winds, trapping fog and mist over the plants. Diffused light aids in the production of the necessary aromatic compounds in the leaves. And the locals have long produced top-quality tea, passing down the methods through generations.

There are certain rituals associated with tea drinking. It is polite to refill others' cups before one's own—and to acknowledge this courtesy by tapping two fingers on the table. In restaurants, removing the lid from the pot, or turning it over, serves to request a refill. And when finished drinking, it is customary to leave one's cup full.

The Cloud Dispersing Pavilion on Mount Huangshan

ANHUI PROVINCE

Mount Huangshan, in the southern part of east China's Anhui Province, is one of the country's best-known scenic locations. It is celebrated for having all the wonders of mountain scenery: spectacular rock peaks, exotically shaped pines, crystal-clear mountain hot springs, and seas of clouds. Scientists believe Huangshan's location was originally an expanse of sea. An eruption of magma caused the granite core of the mountain to form, and later—about 65 million years ago—the slow movement of the Himalayas raised Huangshan to become the mountain it is today.

There are seventy-two distinct peaks in the Huangshan range, two pools, three waterfalls, and twenty-four brooks. Huangshan Mountain itself is composed of three peaks—Lotus Flower Peak, Brightness Summit, and Heavenly Capital. Lianhua (Lotus Flower) Peak is the highest, rising 1,840 meters above sea level. It is named for its shape, which resembles a lotus flower in full bloom, and is surrounded by steep slopes and rocky peaks. On top of the peak is a boat-shaped rock, named Boat for Picking Lotus Seeds. These peaks, with their areas of grotesque rocks, have stimulated the imaginations of millions of scholars, poets, painters, and ordinary visitors throughout China's long history. Even today, the popularity of the area and the climb to the various summits attract countless travelers.

Huangshan scenery is ever-changing; each hour, each day, each season brings new variations to the scene. Beihai Scenic Area, in the central part of the mountain, is a good place to view sunrises and sunsets. Shixin (Seeing is Believing) Peak is the area's most popular tourist spot. It is said that accounts of Huangshan's beauty are unbelievable until you reach this peak; hence the name. Yuping (Jade Screen) Pavilion is located 1,680 meters above sea level. The trees in front of the Jade Screen Pavilion are known as the Guest-greeting and Farewell Pines. From this vantage point, as from the Cloud Dispersing (Pai Yun) Pavilion, pictured here, one can watch the sea of clouds drifting below after it rains, flowing like waterfalls, while the mountain peaks are swathed in mist.

Sea of Clouds on Mount Huangshan

ANHUI PROVINCE

For centuries, many people have considered Mount Huangshan to be the most scenically spectacular mountain in China. The first known reference to it, in the ancient *Shanhai jin* (Book of Mountains and Seas), called it by the name San-tianzi Du. Later writers renamed it Youshan and Yishan. In June of the year 747, a Tang Dynasty emperor decreed that the mountain be called Huangshan (Yellow Mountain). That decree drew public attention to the mountain— it became a focus for poets and painters, and by the Yuan Dynasty (1271–1368), some sixty-four temples had been built there. In 1990, Mount Huangshan was designated a World Heritage site by UNESCO.

Huangshan is home to a broad variety of life. There are some 300 species of vertebrate animals (including asiatic black bears, rhesus and stump-tailed macaques, and clouded leopards), and more than 1,600 species of plants. The site's rock formations include forests of stone pillars, caves and gorges, striated boulders, and individual rocks so grotesquely shaped as to have individual names,

such as "stone monkey," and "pig-headed monk eating watermelon." Scattered among the seventy-two distinct peaks of the Huangshan mountain range are also lakes, waterfalls, and hot springs— including the Cinnabar Hotspring, which is one of the four wonders of Mount Huangshan.

Still, for all its biodiversity and geologic splendor, one of the most breathtaking sights on Mount Huangshan is composed largely of air. The haunting Sea of Clouds is an almost ever-present feature of Huangshan's scenery. The climatic conditions in the region are monsoonal, with an average 70 percent humidity year-round—an environment very conducive to fog and mist. The mists enveloping Huangshan creep into the chasms between the peaks and hang there, as if caught momentarily in the trees. The lookout station pictured here allows visitors to observe in relative comfort as the scene shifts, revealing this or that peak and obscuring others in a manner that has caught the imagination of Huangshan devotees for centuries.

Fengxian Temple, Longmen Grottoes

BUDDHIST CAVE TEMPLES and grottoes can be found at nineteen different sites in China, and of these, three are the most famous by far: the Mogao Grottoes at Dunhuang, the Yungang Grottoes in Shanxi Province, and the Longmen Grottoes. The Longmen Grottoes are located in Henan Province, 13 kilometers south of the city of Luoyang, where the Yihe River cuts a swath through the rocky cliffs, dividing them into Longmen Hill on the west and Xiangshan Hill on the east. The statuary caves of Longmen are cut into a kilometer-long stretch of cliff faces that extends from north to south on both sides of the river. The site encompasses more than 2,100 grottoes and niches, 100,000 statues, 3,600 steles and tablets with carved inscriptions, and 40 pagodas.

Construction of the Longmen Grottoes began in the year 493, when the capital of the Northern Wei Dynasty was moved to Luoyang. The work continued for over four hundred years, spanning the later Northern Qi, Sui, Tang, and Northern Song dynasties.

Of all the cave temples in the Longmen Grottoes, Fengxian (Revered Ancestor) Temple was built on the grandest scale. At 36 meters wide and 41 meters deep, it is the largest open-air shrine at the site. The chief icon of the Fengxian Temple is the seated Vairocana Buddha, pictured here. This carved figure is 17.14 meters high; its head is 4 meters tall, and its ears are almost 2 meters long. This statue has been called "the Venus of the East." With its full cheeks, long, deep eyes, and the barest hint of a smile, the figure's face is uncommonly lifelike. In fact, historical records suggest that the sculpture may have been modeled after a living person—Empress Wu Zetian, who once donated twenty thousand strings of copper coins, each containing one thousand coins, to the Fengxian Temple.

In addition to their importance as a showcase of Buddhist art, the Longmen Grottoes also house ancient clothing, musical instruments, medical implements, calligrapher's tools, and other artifacts relating to the artistic and cultural development of early Chinese society. For these reasons, as well as for their scenic beauty, the Longmen Grottoes are protected by a special agency founded by the Chinese government— the Luoyang International Longmen Grottoes Research and Protection Institute.

Taklimakan Desert

THE TARIM RIVER BASIN, which occupies the southern part of the climatically extreme Xinjiang Uygur Autonomous Region, is one of the largest internal drainage basins in the world. Bordered on the north by the Tianshan (Heavenly) Mountains, and on the west and south by the Kunlun and Altun Mountains, the basin is largely taken up by a desert called Taklimakan. *Taklimakan* is a name any desert should carry proudly—it derives from an expression in a minority language, meaning, "One can go in, but never come out."

Not all deserts are identical; the different types are distinguished by such features as the composition of the ground and the amount of vegetation. Taklimakan is a shifting-sand desert, and it is the second largest of this type anywhere in the world, after the Ar-rub Al-khali desert on the Arabian Peninsula. With an area of roughly 337,000 square kilometers, it is also the largest desert in China. It consists of moving sand dunes in various shapes—crescentic, linear, dome- and star-shaped—averaging 100 to 150 meters in height. Mineral analysis has determined that much of Taklimakan's sand is bedrock weathered from the bordering mountains, deposited into the Tarim basin by rivers and floods.

Local legends tell of demons in the desert guarding vast treasure hordes, and some natives claim to have stumbled upon such places. In a metaphorical sense, this may be true: beneath the desert are valuable resources including oil, natural gas, and minerals. The "demons" of hot winds and freezing cold (the temperature ranges from 50°C in the daytime to –30°C at night) protect these treasures from harvesting.

Another set of treasures has been discovered as well. The region was once fertile, a center of Buddhist civilization. The Swede Sven Hedin, one of the first explorers to cross the Taklimakan alive, discovered the ruins of several cities on the desert's south side in 1895. These discoveries lured other archaeologists, including Britain's Sir Aurel Stein and Germany's Albert von Le Coq, who looted as much as they studied, sending ancient manuscripts home to their own countries' museums. The most recent successful crossing of the Taklimakan was undertaken in 1993–94—an Anglo-Chinese cooperative venture led by Charles Blackmore.

In 1978, several four-thousand-year-old dessicated corpses were discovered under the desert, well-preserved by the sterile climate. The physical features of these corpses mark them as Caucasian—a mystery that has greatly intrigued anthropologists. The current favored theory suggests these people were migrants from southern Russia, as they used burial mounds similar to Russian *kurgans* to lay their dead to rest.

Stone Forest

OF ALL THE MULTIFARIOUS varieties of landscape that nature has produced on this planet, karst formations such as the Stone Forest in China's Yunnan Province are one of the most astonishing to behold. Staring up at those jagged peaks of rock that erupt out of the ground like trees, it is almost possible to forget that one is still on Earth, and to believe that one is viewing an alien landscape firsthand.

The Stone Forest began to form some 270 million years ago, when the movement of the Earth's tectonic plates caused the limestone bed of a vast sea to rise up above the water. Exposure to heavy rain and wind gradually eroded much of the rock, leaving behind the jagged, naturally sculpted peaks one sees today.

Yunnan's Stone Forest is roughly 27,000 hectares in area, of which 80 hectares have been opened as a public scenic area, with trails just over 5,000 meters long. The pinnacles of limestone in that region range from a few meters to several dozen meters in height, and are crowded so close together that they do indeed resemble a forest. Historical records show that the site has been a famous scenic area since the Ming Dynasty (1368–1644).

Although some tourist accommodations such as paths, bridges, railings, and signs have been added to the site—visitors are greeted at the entrance by a huge rock screen on which the words "Stone Forest" are engraved in an ancient Han Dynasty style of calligraphy—it is still possible to get a sense of what it must be like to visit the more remote, untouched areas of the Stone Forest. Scattered between the stone peaks are pools of colored and crystal-clear water, and rock caverns carved out by underground rivers. Scenic spots bear names such as "Moon Lake," "Sword Peak Pond," "Dadie Waterfall," "Lotus Blossom Peak," and "Subterranean Stone Forest in Zhiyun Cave."

Ashma, in the Stone Forest

YUNNAN PROVINCE

THE STONE FOREST—the exotic landscape of limestone peaks that rise sharply out of the ground like trees, as if drawn up by a mystical force—looks from a distance to be a most harsh and forbidding terrain. For all the scenic beauty of its pools, caverns, and rock formations, it seems a dead place; no abundance of vegetation presents itself to the eye. Therefore it comes as something of a surprise to learn that the Stone Forest is inhabited by a native tribe.

The Sani minority, a branch of the Yi ethnic group, call the Stone Forest home. The Sani are noted for their industry, their skill as craftspeople, their warm hospitality, and their festive songs and dances. They weave brightly colored headdresses and exquisitely embroidered clothing, and they sing and dance each day at sunset—particularly the young people. It is not uncommon for them to invite tourists to join them in their high-spirited "Axi Dance Under Moonlight," and the tourists who accept this invitation invariably come away with fond memories of the occasion.

On June 24th of each year, the Sani celebrate their Torchlight Festival, filling the entire Stone Forest with a jovial air. In the early part of the evening, they entertain themselves with performances such as bullfighting and wrestling. Then, as the evening darkens, young men carrying torches chase merrily through the darkness after young women to propose marriage.

In Sani legends, the huge karst peaks of the Stone Forest are said to be the incarnations of people from the distant past—frequently ancient tribal heroes who battled the flood demons. One of the best-known rocks is called Ashma rock. According to legend, a beautiful girl named Ashma was transformed into this peak.

Seven-Star Cave

GUANGXI ZHUANG AUTONOMOUS REGION

ONE OF THE MOST remarkable forms of natural scenery in the southwestern part of China are the karst peaks and caverns, such as those scattered along the Lijiang River. Two of the most famous karst caves are Seven-Star Cave (Qixingyan) and Reed Flute Cave (Ludiyan), located to the east of the city of Guilin, in Guangxi Zhuang Autonomous Region.

These scenic caves were formed over a period of many millions of years, as water erosion created fissures, sinkholes, underground streams, and eventually massive caverns in the region's limestone peaks. The longest known karst cavern zigzags nine kilometers deep into the rock, and the largest has a volume of more than 20,000 cubic meters.

The stalactites, stalagmites, stone slabs and pillars, and other such exotic geological formations are the highlights of the caves' mystique. People have seen such varied shapes among the rock formations as pagodas, human- and animal-shaped figures, bamboo shoots, flowers, and trees.

Seven-Star Cave, located in the western face of Putuo Hill, is also known as the Sun's Resting Place and Bi Xu cave, and has been a popular tourist attraction for centuries, since the Sui and Tang dynasties. The name "Seven-Star Cave" derives from the surrounding limestone peaks, whose arrangement resembles the seven stars that make up the constellation of Ursa Major (the Great Bear). The cave extends almost a kilometer in depth, and maintains a natural temperature of 20°C (68°F) year round. In places along the length of its navigable underground waterway hangs a haunting mist, through which one can discern more than forty intriguing rock formations. These formations have, over the years, acquired such colorful names as: the "Golden Lion," the "Jade Rabbit," the "Jumping Carp," the "Pandas Frolicking over the Stone Ball," the "Pheasant Waiting for the Rabbit," the "Silver Snake," the "Two Snakes Crawling out of One Hole," and the "Supernatural Turtle." Seven Star Cave itself is sometimes referred to as the Cave Abode of the Immortals.

The colored lights that contribute to the cave's air of fantasy were installed to enhance the tourist experience, as part of a state decision that Guilin should consider tourism one of its major industries.

Grotto No. 45, Mogao Grottoes

THE MOGAO GROTTOES in Dunhuang City, Gansu Province, were hewn into a 1,600-meter-long stretch of rock on the eastern slope of Mingsha Mountain, located in a rare mountain gully running from south to north through the barren region. This five-story group of Buddhist cave temples, also called the Thousand-Buddha Cliff, is the largest group of extant grottoes in China and is world-famous as a treasure trove of ancient architecture, murals, and painted statues.

Dunhuang, a small town at the edge of the Gobi desert, was the hub of the so-called Silk Road of medieval and later history. Here, at an oasis in the midst of a harsh desert, was the pivot of caravans going east and west. Not surprisingly, the valley with its greenery at the foot of the cliffs came to be an important place.

According to legend, creation of the Mogao Grottoes began in A.D. 366, when a monk named Yue Zun dug the first cave and also cut a statue of the Buddha into the sandstone cliff face. By the Tang Dynasty, more than one thousand grottoes had been completed, which were expanded under the next several dynasties, until the Yuan. Nearly 750 caves remain today, with 45,000 square meters of murals and about 2,500 painted figures. The largest cave is 40 meters high, and the smallest is just one-third of a meter.

When in the fourteenth century Dunhuang was abandoned, the monks sealed off many of the excavated areas, thus preserving what was left of the contents, including a great library of manuscripts. About sixty thousand manuscripts and other printed documents were discovered in a secret sealed-up cave at the end of the nineteenth century. These items are now preserved in Beijing, Paris, London, and St. Petersburg. A good representation of these is the Stein collection at the British Library, which includes the world's earliest printed book, the Diamond Sutra (dated A.D. 868). The collection of Dunhuang manuscripts in the National Library of China has over ten thousand scrolls.

The Mogao Grottoes were designated as a World Heritage site by UNESCO in 1987.

Grotto No. 285, Mogao Grottoes

THE "THOUSAND BUDDHA CLIFF," as the Mogao Grottoes are sometimes called, includes three monastery-type caves. These have pyramidal ceilings and flat central areas, similar to the rock-cut Ajanta cave monasteries in India. Grotto No. 285 is the largest of these three. It was hewn during the Western Wei Dynasty, and is one of the very few caves that can be dated with precision. Some of the artwork in the cave was dated 538 and 539 by the artists.

The murals in the cave include such legendary figures as the god Fuxi, a ruler of remote antiquity, and the goddess Nuwa, the Spirit of Water. These two appear in flight on the southern slope of the ceiling, chasing after a cintamani jewel, against a background painted like the sky with trailing wisps of cloud. These two serpent-tailed immortals were frequently portrayed as a married couple, their lower bodies wrapped around each other. They are accompanied on the ceiling by many other creatures, including a human-headed Longevity Bird, a thunder god, and other winged spirits and birds, some being ridden by immortals from Taoist legend.

In the west wall, there is a central niche with a seated Buddha inside. The niche is 2.6 meters high, 2 meters wide, and 1 meter deep, with a lintel above that reaches up to the ceiling. The sculpture is executed in exquisite detail, down to the folds of his robe and the fastening of his inner garment. He is attended by rows of Bodhisattvas, also delicately carved. Also on the west wall are pictured elements of ancient Chinese legends, not drawn from Buddhism.

As is appropriate to a monastery-type cave, the guiding theme behind much of the artwork seems to be one of meditation. Hermits are pictured in solitude, and in tranquil wilderness settings where the animals are not disturbed by their presence. Some of the paintings are done in a highly formal, sacerdotal style; others are landscape-oriented, and still others are narrative, depicting stories from myth and legend.

Dazu Grottoes

CHONGQING MUNICIPALITY

THE NAME *DAZU* TRANSLATES to "Big Foot," referring to a legend of Buddha's leaving his footprints on some of the region's rocks. Regardless of the legend's literal truth, the Buddhist faith has certainly left its mark. While not quite as famous as the grottoes at Dunhuang, Yungang, and Longmen, the art of the Dazu Grottoes appeared later, and, for that reason, was in some ways more sophisticated. Also, because they were constructed over a long span of time—from the Northern and Southern Dynasties (420–581), through the Tang Dynasty (618–907), through the Five Dynasties (907–960), and the Song Dynasty (960–1279)—they serve to catalogue the evolution of Chinese grotto art during its later period.

The grottoes are spread out across several dozen sites on four mountains in Dazu County, Chongqing Municipality. Altogether, there are several hundred grottoes and niches containing over sixty thousand Buddhist sculptures. The largest, best-known, and most skillfully done grottoes are located on Baoding (Treasure Peak) and Beishan (Northern) Mountains.

Beishan, also known as Dragon Mound Hill, became a military base in the year 892, whereupon the commanding general commissioned the first Buddhist carvings. The work continued for more than 250 years. The best-known carving on Beishan is the Xinshenche (Wheel of the Universe) Cave, in which eight Bodhisattvas arranged around a central Buddha depict the cycle of human life.

The three statues in the photo are saints from the Huayen sect of Buddhism, each seven meters high, located on Baodingshan. The Baodingshan carvings were created between 1179 and 1249, along a stretch of cliffs 400 meters long. Unlike the haphazardly organized Beishan carvings, Baodingshan follows an overarching plan dictated by a Buddhist monk named Zhao Zhifeng. In places, the long cliff reads like a narrative scroll, the successive sculptures acting out religious and historical stories. The most remarkable sculpture on Baodingshan is Reclining Buddha. Measuring 31 meters long and 5 meters high, surrounded on three sides by devotees, this statue depicts Buddha as he enters Nirvana. Also in the caves at Baodingshan is the thousand-armed gilded Goddess of Mercy, an eye in each hand.

The figures dating from the Tang Dynasty tend to have full, round, and ingenuous-looking faces. Those from the Five Dynasties look more delicate, with a keen intelligence visible in their features. And the Song Dynasty sculptures are the most glamorous, with attractive bodies and exquisite clothing. The Dazu figures tend to incorporate realistic, human attributes into the divine beings portrayed, and depict scenes from everyday life—a relatively late development in the evolution of grotto art.

Yungang Grottoes

THE PRACTICE OF CARVING TEMPLES out of rock originated with the Buddhists in India, but was taken up enthusiastically by the Chinese. The most famous groups of grottoes in China are the Mogao Grottoes in Dunhuang, the Longmen Grottoes in Luoyang, and the Yungang Grottoes in Shanxi Province.

The Yungang Grottoes are located 16 kilometers west of the city of Datong, at the southern foot of Mount Wuzhou. They are cut in a honeycomb pattern, which evidences the fact that a certain amount of planning went into this artistic endeavor. The grottoes stretch a full kilometer along the mountain, from east to west. There are a total of fifty-three grottoes at this site, and they contain some fifty-one thousand sculptures in the form of statues and low relief carvings.

After the Northern Wei Dynasty emperor Taiwu (Taiwu Di) spent five years persecuting the Buddhist faith from the years of 444 to 449, Buddhists persuaded his successor to order the construction of five great cave shrines. The emperor gave the responsibility for creating the Yungang Grottoes to a Buddhist monk named Tan Yao. The construction of the grottoes began in the year 453, and, although renovations and minor additions continued through many of the following dynasties, the majority of the work had really been completed by the year 495, a mere forty-two years after it began.

The basic structure of the caves appears to have been modeled after the Mogao Grottoes, whose construction had already begun one hundred years earlier. However, the Yungang Grottoes are remarkable in their own right, particularly for the extraordinary variety of themes depicted in the artwork there. In addition to the traditional representations of Buddhas, disciples, and flying fairies, there are birds, animals, and even miniatures of pagodas. The earliest artwork displays strong western influences, in the form of Persian and Byzantine weapons, Greek tridents, lions, acanthus leaves, and men with beards. In the later sculptures, a more uniquely Chinese influence can be found: there are dragons, bodhisattvas, and flying *apsaras*, or heavenly beings.

Buddhist Statues at Yungang Grottoes

THE YUNGANG GROTTOES stretch a full kilometer along the southern face of Wuzhou Mountain. Along that stretch, the caves can be divided into three major sections. In the west, there are a total of five rock caves. These earliest grottoes are oval-shaped, and were planned on a large scale. The main statue in this group is 17 meters high, a serene seated Buddha accompanied by a disciple. The walls of his chamber are carved in low relief of great delicacy, which appears all the more spectacular in contrast to the enormous size of the Buddha itself.

In the central stretch of grottoes, the caves are oblong in shape, and each one consists of two chambers. This was an innovation of the Northern Wei Dynasty emperor Wencheng, the second person to hold the title of Emperor while the grottoes were being built. His predecessor had begun the process of allowing images of the previous emperors to be placed in the caves. Emperor Wencheng altered this practice by opening twin caves, one for each parent of the emperor being honored. Some caves even include a third adjoining chamber for a representation of the living emperor. The walls, arches, and roofs of the central grottoes are covered with low relief carvings of Buddhist themes.

The eastern grottoes are square in shape, each with a delicately sculpted central column in the shape of a pagoda that reaches all the way to the ceiling. On the walls of the eastern caves are carved niches with Buddhist statues enshrined within. A particularly remarkable achievement in the art of the Yungang Grottoes is the carving of the entire *Jataka,* or life story, of Sakyamuni Buddha, from his birth to the time he attained Buddhahood, on the walls and central pagoda pillar of one of these caves.

The Buddhist statues pictured here are in the open air, outside the entrance to one of the caves in the central section of the Yungang Grottoes. The main statue of Sakyamuni in this group of sculptures is 13.7 meters tall.

Jiuzhaigou (Nine-Village Valley)

SICHUAN PROVINCE

ACCORDING TO LEGEND, the warrior-god Dage once created a magic mirror, and gave it as a gift to the goddess Wunosemo. A mischievous imp caused her to drop the mirror, and it fell from the heavens to Earth, where it shattered into more than a hundred pieces, and each piece became a resplendent lake.

Waters, in every form, are the pride of Jiuzhaigou (Nine-Village Valley). Located in Nanping County in the northern part of Sichuan Province (about 400 kilometers north of the provincial capital, Chengdu), Jiuzhaigou is a mountain gorge in the southern part of the Minshan Mountain range. More than 40 kilometers long, and covering more than 60,000 hectares of land, the valley offers a gorgeous variety of lakes, waterfalls, springs, and streams.

Many of the lakes are classic ribbon lakes, dammed by natural occurrences such as rockfalls from avalanches, their waters tinctured vibrant emerald, light yellow, and sapphire colors by chemicals leached from the mountains' sedimentary rock. The waterfalls of Jiuzhaigou, too, are among China's finest, including Xiongmaohai (Panda Lake) Fall, which plummets a depth of 78 meters in three steps, Zhengzhutan (Pearl Shoal) Fall, a 310-meter-wide curtain of water 8.5 meters high, and the spectacular Norilang Falls, enlivened by seasonal accents of color as flowering trees come into bloom.

The region is also home to a number of endangered species, including giant pandas (whose population is estimated at between fifteen and twenty individuals), golden snub-nosed monkeys, white-lipped deer, and takins. The region's cool temperate climate remains pleasant for animals and people year-round, ranging from just below freezing in the winter to just below 70°F (21°C) in the summer. Northern and southern types of vegetation meet at this latitude; broad-leafed trees and evergreens grow together, each adding to the beauty of the land.

Jiuzhaigou acquired its name, "Nine-Village Valley," because it once hosted nine Tibetan villages. Of these, six now remain, with a total population of about one thousand people. Agricultural activity dominates village life; yaks are raised for milk and meat, and used as work animals to cultivate the fields, and there are mills powered by water wheels.

Jiuzhaigou was designated as a World Heritage site by UNESCO in 1992.

West Lake

Zhejiang Province

As an old Chinese saying goes "There is heaven above, Suzhou and Hangzhou below." Marco Polo agreed, once calling Hangzhou the most enchanting city in all the world.

Hangzhou is a city with over 2,100 years of history. It is a renowned exporter of fine silk and teas, and the current capital of Zhejiang Province. Hangzhou owes its fame as a scenic spot largely to Xizi Hu, also known as West Lake, the large, picturesque, and tranquil lagoon on the city's western edge.

The lake spans six square kilometers of surface area, and is, on the average, 1.5 meters deep. In ancient times, West Lake was a shallow sea gulf, but later separated from the sea, developing into a "residual" lake. Surrounded on three sides by rolling, wooded hills and mountains, the lake's shoreline also features the National Tea and Silk Museums, and the Huqingyutang Therapeutic Center of Traditional Chinese Medicine. The lake also holds islets, walkways, bridges, and pavilions.

At the center of West Lake are the three islets known as Lesser Yingzhou, Mid-Lake Pavilion, and Ruangong Isle. Su Causeway—named after the poet Su Dongpo (A.D. 1037–1101)—bisects the lake from north to south, and Bai Causeway—named for the poet Bai Juyi (A.D. 772–846)—allows access from the city to Solitary Hill, on the northern shore of the lake.

Other sights of interest on West Lake include Broken Bridge (part of the Bai Causeway), Leifeng Tower, Crooked Courtyard, Calm Lake, Flowers Harbor, and Nanping Hill. The surrounding hills are home to exotically shaped peaks and serene forests and springs, offering scenes to supplement those of the lake. The lake is also surrounded by carefully manicured parks, with blossoming flowers and beautiful trees, such as the willows in this photo.

The Song Dynasty poet Su Shi once compared the lake to a Chinese beauty named Xizi:

Rippling water shimmering on a sunny day;
Misty mountains wonder in the rain;
Plain or gaily decked out like Xizi;
the West Lake is always alluring.

It was from this poem that West Lake came to be known also as Xizi Lake.

Lake Taihu

JUST OUTSIDE THE CITY OF WUXI in coastal Jiangsu Province, near the border of Zhejiang Province, and just south of the Yangtze Delta, lies one of the four largest lakes in China, and one of the most famous. Lake Taihu, the nation's third largest freshwater lake, with a surface area of more than 2,400 square kilometers and a shoreline over 480 kilometers in circumference, is one of the chief attractions of the town.

The lake's vast waters and lovely shoreline gardens have, for centuries, provided subject matter for painters and inspiration for poets. Its shores are dotted with dozens of small towns and villages where the main occupation is fishing. Some villagers use bamboo poles to seal off 50-square-meter areas of water for enclosed fish farming. In fact, Lake Taihu produces fully a quarter of China's freshwater fish.

The city of Wuxi, founded three thousand years ago during the Han Dynasty (206 B.C.– A.D. 220), retains some measure of quaint antique charm with its cobbled streets and network of canals. However, beginning with the construction of the Grand Canal through the center of Wuxi in the sixth century A.D., the city also became a center for industry and foreign trade. Today, Wuxi houses 4.3 million people, and is known by the nickname "Little Shanghai."

In addition to the production of silks, cotton, and food products such as flour and vegetable oils, the towns of the Taihu Lake basin entertain some 14 million tourists each year. A favorite outing is to take a boat to the Taihu Fairy Islands–also called the Turtle Islets–in the center of the lake. Once known as the Sanshan (Three Mounts) Islands, these three small land masses–covering a total of two hectares– are linked, and together form a contour that resembles a giant turtle floating on the surface of the water. To the islets' natural charm have been added many attractions in the style of classic Chinese architecture, including the White Marble Screen Wall of the Jade Emperor, the Water Screened Cave, the Hill of Flowers and Fruits, the Pavilion of Affectionate Couples, and the Immortal Cave.

Since industry is dependent on the canals, village life centers around fishing. And with tourists and local artists attracted to the lake's beauty, life in the Taihu Lake basin is linked inextricably to the water.

Zhaoling Mausoleum

LIAONING PROVINCE

THE CITY OF SHENYANG is China's fifth largest city, and the capital of northeastern Liaoning Province. Zhaoling Mausoleum, located on Jiujun Hill in the northern part of Shenyang, is the most scenically beautiful locale in the city.

Zhaoling, also called Beiling (Northern Tomb), is the mausoleum of Emperor Taizong of the Qing Dynasty and his empress, Xiao Duan Wen. Construction of the mausoleum took eight years, beginning in 1643 and reaching completion in 1651. With a total area of 180,000 square meters and a circumference of 60 kilometers, Zhaoling is the largest of the three Qing tombs north of Shanhaiguan Pass. In addition to the emperor and empress, the mausoleum includes the companion graves of more than two hundred court officials and military officers who served the emperor. Some forty-five inscribed memorial tablets have been preserved in the Zhaoling Tomb Museum.

The mausoleum is built along an axis that runs from south to north. At the southern end is Zhenghongmen, a red building with a yellow tiled roof, which serves as entrance gate. One travels through the first courtyard along a path that is reminiscent of the Ming Tombs, in that it is flanked on both sides by stone columns and sculptures of animals. Two of the animals immortalized in stone are white horses named Dabai (Great White) and Xiaobai (Little White)—the emperor's favorites. As the path leads farther north, one encounters structures such as the Sacred Virtue Stele, the Hall of Sacrifices, the square tomb enclosure surrounded by battlements with corner towers, the entrance gate Long'en Men, the large hall Long'en Dian, and Minglou Tower. From the height of the tower, the grave mound is visible, surrounded by a semicircular lawn.

Emperor Taizong was one of the great emperors in Chinese history. His reign was a prosperous one, due in large part to a series of policies he instituted, known as the reforms of the Zhenguan reign. Agriculture, crafts, and trade all flourished, and there were great advances in the technologies used for textile production, shipbuilding, metalwork, and the manufacturing of porcelain.

Although it was forbidden in imperial times for commoners to set foot on imperial burial grounds, the mausoleum has since been restored and maintained, enlarged, and opened as a public park (Beiling Park).

Cemetery of Confucius

THE HUGE COMPLEX OF MORE than one hundred buildings that commemorate the birthplace of Confucius–the Temple, Cemetery, and family mansion of Confucius–is located at Qufu, in Shandong Province, and occupies a space roughly one-third the size of Qufu town. The Temple was built in 478 B.C., just one year after his death, and has been destroyed and rebuilt several times over the centuries. Dacheng (Great Achievements) Hall, the largest building in the complex, stands 32 meters tall, and is roofed–by special permission of the Ming emperor reigning at the time of its construction–with tiles of imperial yellow like the palaces in Beijing. The Cemetery–also known as the Confucian Woods–includes Confucius' tomb, and the remains of most of his descendants.

Confucius, born in the State of Lu (present-day Shandong Province) in 551 B.C., the child of a deposed noble family, was the most influential philosopher in Chinese history. His system of thought focused on morality and on the philosophy of government. Its two most important concepts were *Ren* (benevolence) and *Yi* (right conduct).

Ren, the fundamental attitude of Confucianism, means simply that one ought to "love others," and therefore behave generously toward them. *Yi,* or moral duty, can be divided into *zhong* (loyalty) and *shu* (reciprocity). *Shu* is similar to what is known in the Western world as the "Golden Rule"–it states, "don't do to others what you would not want yourself." *Zhong,* however, does not mean blind loyalty, but rather, *thoughtful* loyalty. Confucius believed the ideal person should take "as much trouble to discover what is right as lesser men take to discover what will pay." Since an individual's highest duty is not to a master, but to "what is right," the duty of obedience actually includes refusing any order to do what is wrong.

Confucius also had quite a political career. When Confucius was a young man, Duke Zhao of Lu frequently came to him for advice, until his ministers, out of envy or fear, influenced the duke not to seek his counsel any further. Years later, the next Duke of Lu made Confucius a city magistrate. A benevolent and caring ruler, Confucius believed that a ruler should lead by example rather than by force and intimidation. Under his leadership, the city flourished, and he was promoted to Grand Secretary of Justice, and later made Chief Minister of Lu.

Ultimately, he resigned from political office and spent his remaining years traveling throughout China with his students. He never wrote down any of his teachings, but his students did. Their writings, known as the Analects of Confucius, are the only extant record of his thought.

Lake Tianchi (Heavenly Lake)

LAKE TIANCHI (HEAVENLY LAKE) is one of the foremost natural tourist attractions in China. It sits at an elevation of 1,900 meters above sea level, halfway up Bogda Peak (God's Peak). Bogda Peak is a part of the Tianshan Mountain range, to the northeast of Urumqi, the capital city of the Xinjiang Uygur Autonomous Region in China's northwest. The lake is 3,400 meters long and 1,500 meters wide, giving it a total surface area of 4.9 square kilometers. It is 105 meters in depth at its deepest point.

Lake Tianchi is a moraine lake, which is to say that it was formed by a glacier, and it stores melted snow from the surrounding mountains. Its crystal clear waters vary in color from jade green to resplendent deep blue, depending on the light, and the vantage point from which the lake is viewed. Hemmed in by snow-capped mountains whose sunny slopes are covered with evergreen trees—pines, spruces, and cypresses—the lake and its surroundings embody an ideal of beautiful alpine scenery. During the warmer seasons, the land among the trees is further decorated with exotic wildflowers and lush green grasses, and roamed by flocks of sheep.

The lake freezes solid in winter, and part of its appeal for tourists during this season is that it becomes a magnificent outdoor skating rink. In fact, China's winter skating games have been held at the Heavenly Lake.

The Heavenly Lake was known in ancient times as Lake Yaochi (the Jade Lake). According to legend, when King Mu of the Zhou Dynasty traveled to the western part of China, he attended a great banquet hosted by the Golden Mother of Lake Yaochi, also known as the Mother of the Western Skies. This legendary banquet was hosted at Lake Tianchi, which led to its receiving the name of Lake Yaochi.

The Xinjiang Uygur Autonomous Region is located in the central part of the continent, to the west of the Taklimakan Desert. It is the largest among China's provinces and autonomous regions, with a total area of 1,660,000 square kilometers. Its climate is dry and temperate, and it has a population of over 17.18 million people.

For the last two millennia, the area around the city of Urumqi has been populated by farming people, who herd livestock such as cattle and sheep on the pasture lands. Even the name "Urumqi" derives from the Mongolian for "beautiful pastures."

Black Dragon Pool

YUQUAN (JADE SPRING) PARK takes its name from the pool that is its best-known natural feature. The water of Heilong (Black Dragon) Pool appears under the light of day to be a sparkling, lucid green color reminiscent of jade. The entire park, located on Longquan Mountain, about 15 kilometers north of the city of Kunming, is a delightful scenic spot, with swaying willows, cherry trees, and delicate flowers, with mighty peaks such as the Jade Dragon Hill and the Lion Mountain, and with an assortment of temples and pavilions built to complement the scenery.

The city of Kunming, and the land surrounding it, is blessed with a subtropical climate that remains pleasantly temperate and mild throughout the year. In fact, Kunming has earned the nickname "City of Eternal Spring." It is also a region of extreme ethnic diversity, with some twenty-five ethnic groups residing nearby, including the Bai, Hani, Hui, Miao, and Yi. Archaeological evidence suggests that Kunming has been inhabited for as long as 300,000 years, and even the city's known history is more than 2,000 years long.

Beneath the Jade Dragon Snow Peak stands an elegant little pagoda called Deyue (Moon Embracing) Pavilion, beside the Belt Bridge made of white marble. Deyue Pavilion was rebuilt in 1963. Situated next to Deyue Pavilion is Wufeng (Five Phoenix) Pavilion—the main building of Huguo Temple, which was originally built on a faraway mountain, but was later moved to Yuquan Park for the convenience of visitors. Its name derives from the style of its roof, whose overlapping cornices look, from any angle, like a group of five phoenixes preparing to take off in flight.

An old legend tells of a Taoist scholar named Lu Dongbin, a reclusive man living in the mid-eighth century A.D., who, upon mastering the secrets of Taoism, began travelling across China to hunt and slay demons. When he came to Yuquan Park, he discovered that the pool was inhabited by ten evil dragons—terribly dangerous and destructive creatures. According to the legend, he killed nine of these dragons with his sword, and allowed the tenth, a small black dragon, to remain in the pool on the condition that it would work for the benefit of humankind. Black Dragon Pool is therefore named for this one remaining dragon. Lu Dongbin is known still as one of the Eight Immortals of the Taoist faith.

Sunset on Hainan Island

HAINAN PROVINCE

HAINAN ISLAND HAS BEEN known by a variety of nicknames throughout its history. For its location as the southernmost point in China, it has been known as the Tail of the Dragon and the End of the Earth. For its role as a place of exile in imperial times, it has been called Siberia of the Tropics. And for its endless heavenly stretches of beach resorts and its colorful native ethnic populations, it is also known as the Hawaii of the Orient.

Hainan lies in the South China Sea, across Qiongzhou Strait from the mainland's Leizhou Peninsula. With an area of 34,000 square kilometers and a coastline of over 1,500 kilometers, it is China's second largest island, next only to Taiwan. China's youngest province, Hainan was granted provincial status–and special economic freedoms– in 1988, in the hope of using its natural resources and tourism potential to the fullest. Hainan is also strategically important; as China's southernmost coastal region, it serves as the nation's window on the south seas, a center of naval communications.

The capital city of Hainan Province is Haikou. More relaxed than most provincial capitals, this city on the island's north coast is not much more than a point of arrival and departure. Its only real points of interest are Five Figures Temple and Hai Rui's Tomb, both commemorating individuals exiled to this tropical paradise by ancient emperors.

Coming to Hainan without traveling to the beaches of Sanya is like going to Hollywood and not thinking about movies. This southern city boasts everything one could want from a beach: pristine white sands, azure skies, palm and coconut trees, and warm blue waters. Dadonghai beach is especially popular, but the coast stretches around to encompass such interesting areas as Jingfeng Ling to the west and Lingshui to the east. Jingfeng Ling is a rainforest reserve, protected at the suggestion of UNESCO conservationists, where the island's original vegetation remains undisturbed. Lingshui was home to China's first communist government as early as 1928, and offers ferries to Monkey Island, where researchers study local groups of macaques.

Tongza, in Hainan's central highlands, is home to the island's native Li and Miao ethnic groups. The Li nationality, with a population of nearly 800,000, live only on Hainan. They are talented weavers and embroiderers, with delicious cuisine and intriguing customs. Their name derives from the topknot, or *li,* that was once the common hairstyle among Li men. As recently as the 1930s, they still lived as hunter-gatherers in Hainan's mountains. The Miao nationality were hired as mercenaries to put down a Li rebellion in the eighteenth century; but eventually they stopped fighting and settled in nearby valleys.

Yurts in Axi Pastureland

SICHUAN PROVINCE

UCH OF THE LAND area in Yunnan Province of southwestern China, and the northern Inner Mongolia Autonomous Region, is taken up by grasslands—vast, undulating plains of grass that stretch in every direction as far as the eye can see. Most of these areas are inhabited by one or another of China's many minority tribes, who use the plains as pastureland for their horses, sheep, and yaks.

In Sichuan Province, there is a sharp dichotomy between the modern, densely populated east and the remote and relatively undeveloped west. Western and northern Sichuan Province, in sight of the Litang Peaks, a plain about 900 meters higher than Lhasa in Tibet, is the scene of an annual fair. The town is enlivened by an annual fair in which a tented city springs to life, and horsemen hold races and show off their riding skills to popular enthusiasm.

The Axi people are a branch of the southeastern Yi tribes, believed to have migrated long ago from Azhede in northwestern Sichuan Province to Honghe Prefecture of Yunnan Province. The term "southeastern Yi" is actually somewhat misleading. The nineteen tribes that compose the southeastern Yi were always separate—they were never a single group. Today, there are over 75,000 Axi in China. Their religious ceremonies include energetic rituals to ward off evil spirits, appease the Fire God, and worship the God of Seeds. They have no formal marriage ceremony; each member of a couple does a day or two of ceremonial housework for the parents of his or her betrothed, after which they return home, and are considered married. The Axi language has fifteen vowel sounds and thirty-five consonants, but had no written form until 1986, when scholars in Kunming created one. Even today, few Axi know the written form of their language.

The tents in which grassland tribes live are known as yurts. These simple structures are usually circular and domed, made of a heavy covering of rawhide or canvas-and-felt, supported by a frame of wood or, less frequently, bamboo. Yurts were invented by Mongolian nomadic tribes, who needed a home that was portable enough to be transported by a single beast of burden, yet efficient enough that it could be kept warm during the frigid northern winters. Though the concept comes from Mongolia, the name *yurt* was bestowed by Russian travelers. A Mongol called his tent a *ger*, meaning, simply, "dwelling."

Wild Camels on Barkol Grassland

The Tianshan (Heavenly) Mountain range, running from west to east, separates the dry lands of the Jungar Basin and the Tarim Basin—the two areas that make up most of the Xinjiang Uygur Autonomous Region. At a length of 2,414 kilometers and a width that varies from 320 to 480 kilometers, the Tianshan Mountains take up just over one million square kilometers, an area roughly equal to that of the United States' Rocky Mountains. Most of the precipitation in Xinjiang occurs at high elevations, and the region's moisture is stored in slow-melting glaciers.

Although trade did not begin to develop along the northern branch of the Silk Road until after the seventh century, the road did exist as long ago as the Han Dynasty (206 B.C.– A.D. 220). During those ancient times, the town of Barkol, at the foot of the Tianshan Mountains, was one of the vital communications centers along that route. Many relics typical of Central Plains cultures have been unearthed in the Barkol Grassland. The modern inhabitants of the Tianshan grasslands are predominantly Muslim farmers and herders. The northern slopes of the Tianshan range receive enough water to support green meadows and forests, with populations of hardy wild animals such as horses, yaks, and camels.

There are two species of camel: the Dromedary, or Arabian camel, and the Bactrian camel, which is native to central Asia, from Xinjiang to Mongolia. Some scientists believe the Dromedary camel is a mutation of the Bactrian, as a second hump appears in the early stages of its embryonic development. Bactrian camels are about 1.5 meters tall at the shoulders, with shorter legs and thicker torsos than Dromedaries.

Camels have been domesticated for over three thousand years, and make excellent beasts of burden. They can carry weights as great as one ton, and travel up to 47 kilometers in a single day. They have pouches in their stomachs for storing water, and can go without drinking for up to nine days, although they are not often forced to endure such extreme deprivation. They can tolerate extremes of heat and cold—a necessity in the deserts of Xinjiang, where temperatures range from 50°C to thirty below zero in a single day.

Wild camels are the ancestors of domestic camels; genetic tests have proved that they are not merely domestic runaways. Perhaps as few as seven hundred wild camels remain in Chinese and Mongolian deserts—a 75 percent decrease from the 1991 population. In 1999, the Chinese government designated the area of Lop Nur as a protective sanctuary for wild camels.

The Grand Canal in Suzhou

THE CITY OF SUZHOU is one of China's two "heavenly" cities, according to an ancient saying—"There is Paradise above, Suzhou and Hangzhou below"—and one of China's four most frequently visited tourist towns. Situated on the plains of the Yangtze Delta some fifty miles west of Shanghai, the city was established in the year 514 B.C. It has since become famous as the center of Chinese silk, and revered for its unrivalled classical gardens, including Master of Nets, Wave Pavilion, and the Humble Administrator's Garden. Through the city runs a network of canals, crisscrossing like the lines of a spider's web. These canals, whose presence gives Suzhou its reputation as "the Venice of the East," link the city's many lakes and ponds, eventually joining up with the Grand Canal.

The Grand Canal (Da Yunhe) is the world's longest constructed waterway, dwarfing both the Panama and Suez canals—an impressive feat of engineering surpassed in China only by the Great Wall. Today, in its finished form, the canal stretches nearly 1,800 kilometers, from Beijing in the north to Hangzhou in the south, with twenty-four locks (sections of water closed off by gates) and sixty bridges along the way.

Construction of the Grand Canal began in 486 B.C. during the reign of King Fucai of the State of Wu, most likely for military purposes, when laborers deepened and linked existing rivers. But the lion's share of the credit for the canal belongs to Emperor Yangdi of the Sui Dynasty, who, in the early seventh century A.D., made it his goal to link the two major trading rivers, the Yangtze and the Yellow. This project involved the conscription of nearly six million laborers—in some villages, this meant every able-bodied commoner—who worked under military supervision and would be flogged if they failed to meet work quotas.

The canal was originally intended to transport rice from the fertile Yangtze Delta to the more heavily populated north. Ultimately, it had political ramifications as well. The expansion of trade under the Tang and Song dynasties caused political power to drift south; the Song Dynasty made their capital in Hangzhou, and the Ming later established themselves in Nanjing.

In the early twentieth century, more efficient modes of transport caused the canal to fall into relative disuse. Today, it is no longer used for long-distance journeys, but local industries still use it extensively to move shipments between nearby towns. Long strings of barges, and hasty loading and unloading in docks, are common sights on the canal. Many of the families who work on these barges live in the whitewashed houses that line every waterway.

The Bund

THE BUND IS A 1.5-KILOMETER-LONG boulevard that stretches along the west bank of the Huangpu River in Shanghai. The word *Bund* is an Anglo-Indian term meaning "muddy waterfront." This description is not entirely inappropriate. Shanghai sank several meters between 1920 and 1965, and water had to be pumped back into the ground to keep the situation from becoming more severe. Today, though, with its combination of river scenery, architectural styles, commerce, and street performers, the Bund has become a favorite destination for tourists in Shanghai.

The Bund was once a mere ten meters wide, and lined with sycamores, cedars, cassias, and camphor trees. On the east side of the street, some of the vestiges of this natural charm can still be found. Looking out to the east, one can see the sailing vessels gliding along the glittering waves of the river, letting out blasts from their horns, beyond the forest of masts formed by the boats in dock. On the shore, well-maintained lawns, flower beds, and lines of flowering trees add beautiful bright colors to the promenade. Huangpu Park, in particular, is a pleasant place to relax and enjoy the scenery. The park used to be notorious for signs that read, "Prohibited to dogs and Chinese," but those signs have long since been removed.

On its west side, the Bund resembles nothing so much as a showcase of international architecture. This is where much of the commercial trading in Shanghai was conducted during the early decades of the twentieth century. At that time, the Bund was home to a great many foreign businessmen. Many of the buildings date from this era: former banks and trading houses of neoclassical designs reminiscent of New York and Chicago. The Customs House, seen here to the left, is constructed in an English Tudor style, with a clock that chimes like London's Big Ben. Also pictured, nearer the center of the photo, is the Peace Hotel, one of the most famous hotels in China.

Victoria Harbor

HONG KONG

TOURISM IN MUCH OF MAINLAND China is a matter of looking into the past—viewing ancient temples and pagodas, centuries-old imperial mausoleums and palaces, and timeless landscapes. But tourism—and, for that matter, life—in Hong Kong exists in the unrelenting, frenetic present. Seen from a distance, Hong Kong's skyline is an unbroken array of skyscrapers and neon signs—more modern, and in ways more impressive, than even Manhattan's. Seen from up close, the city is one of the world's foremost centers of international business, and its lifestyle is one of fast-paced capitalism and dizzying energy.

Hong Kong learned the power of free trade the hard way. British merchants came to the region in the late seventeenth century, and had great success trading opium for commodities such as silk, spices, and silver. The Qing Dynasty realized that they were losing valuable resources in exchange for addictive drugs, and placed restrictions on British trade. When smugglers continued bringing in even greater quantities of the drug, the Qing resolved to stop the opium trade altogether. They seized a British shipload of opium and ceremonially burned it—an outrage that precipitated the Opium Wars. British naval blockades and assaults on Chinese ports forced China into the Treaty of Nanking and later the Treaty of Peking, granting Britain dominion over Hong Kong, Kowloon, and the New Territories. Not until 1997 did Britain willingly relinquish sovereignty over the region. Today, Hong Kong is a Special Administrative Region of China.

Hong Kong (its name derived from the Cantonese for "fragrant harbor") is also a city of contradictions. The prevalent clothing and hairstyles are positively Western; the city's per capita GNP has doubled in just a decade; and nestled among its gleaming skyscrapers is the densest concentration of shopping malls anywhere on Earth, and no small number of McDonald's restaurants. But underneath that glossy exterior, the spirit of old China remains. Some 97 percent of the populace are of Chinese descent—particularly Cantonese—and the vast majority speak only Chinese. Even the leaders of multinational corporations leave work in the evening to eat dinners of roast duck and worship in traditional Buddhist temples.

Victoria Harbor, pictured here, lies in the heart of the city, just off the northern shore of Hong Kong Island. In the days when the majority of foreign commercial traffic arrived via the water, Victoria Harbor served as the island's main port. Seen from Victoria Peak to the south, the modern harbor illuminated at night by the city lights is a dazzling panorama.

Harbin Ice Lantern Festival

HEILONGJIANG PROVINCE

ARBIN IS THE CAPITAL city of Heilongjiang Province, the northern-most region of China. The name *Harbin* means "drying fishnets" in the Manchurian dialect. The city started out as a small fishing village, but its proximity to Russia caused rapid growth, due to the construction of the Russian Manchurian Railroad (also known as the Chinese Eastern Railway). The first immigrants were merchants and railway engineers, who were shortly followed by a flood of refugees escaping from the Russian Revolution. Architecturally, Harbin is perhaps the most Russian city outside of the former Soviet Union, with traditional onion domes forming much of its skyline, and has been nicknamed the Moscow of the East.

Harbin's other, even better-known nickname is the City of Ice. Each year, beginning on New Year's Day and lasting into mid-February, the city's attention turns to Zhaolin Park, near the south bank of the Songhua River. The park plays host to one of the world's most spectacular traditions: the Harbin Ice Lantern Festival.

Long ago, northern fishermen used hollowed-out blocks of ice as lampshades to shield their candles from the wind. From this practice developed the art of *bingdiao,* ice carving. Artists would create hollow ice blocks in a variety of shapes, using molds, and place candles inside. They organized the first ice lantern show in 1963, and it was such a success that it turned into an annual tradition. In the years since its inception, the festival has attracted more than twenty-five million visitors from around the world.

Naturally, the sculptures have grown more elaborate each year. Sculptors start with blocks of ice cut from the Songhua River, which freezes solid to a great depth in the northern cold, typically between $-20°$ and $-30°C$ all winter. Using chainsaws, picks, and chisels, they carve exquisite sculptures—entire land-scapes of mountains and trees, inhabited by ice animals, birds, human figures, and crystalline fish in frozen pools; ambitious ice cities, featuring pavil-ions, towers, bridges, and palaces; and even scenes taken from theater, opera, and, more recently, science fiction. Whereas once the sculptures were lit with candles, these days the blocks of ice contain neon lights in pink, green, blue, and purple. For anyone who loves fantasy novels and yearns to walk around in a real-life Wonderland, this is the place to be.

Xiaoling Mausoleum

THE ANCIENT CHINESE EMPERORS' belief in the immortality of the soul is evidenced in the great effort and endless resources that they devoted to making their tombs as extravagant as their palaces. Like the Ming Tombs at the foot of Tianshou Mountain near Beijing, Xiaoling Mausoleum, where the founding emperor of the Ming Dynasty, Zhu Yuanzhang, was buried with his empress, is an excellent example of this phenomenon. It is one of the largest extant royal tombs in China.

Xiaoling Mausoleum was built at the southern slope of Zhongshan Mountain, near Nanjing, in 1381, before the Ming Dynasty moved its capital to Beijing, and therefore is geographically distant from the thirteen Ming Tombs known as *Shisanling*. However, there are certain similarities of design between the two sites. The approach to the mausoleum is a road known as the Sacred Way. Flanking that path are stone statues arranged in pairs—of animals (lions, camels, elephants, horses, and mythical beasts called *xiezhi* and *qilin*), military officers, and officials of the royal court. Behind those figures once stood additional buildings of the tomb, including a Hall of Enjoyment, a Walled Palace, and a Citadel of Treasures. Beneath the latter building, the burial chamber lay underground. Most of the buildings of Xiaoling Mausoleum were destroyed long ago; however, there remains a pavilion known as the Square City. So named for its resemblance to a citadel, this structure houses an 8.87-meter-high memorial tablet commissioned by the emperor's son Chengzu.

Zhu Yuanzhang was born in 1328, the son of a poor peasant family. He was orphaned at the age of sixteen and went to live in a Buddhist monastery. He left the monastery eight years later to join a band of rebels, and quickly became their leader. In 1356 he captured Nanjing, the capital of Jiangsu Province. Nanjing was a strategically valuable site, guarded by hills and rivers, with a location on the Yangtze River that made it a center for trade. Having consolidated his power in this region, he moved on to capture Beijing in 1368, proclaiming himself emperor under the reign name "Hungwu," and founding the Ming Dynasty in the process. By 1382 he had ended the rule of the Mongol Yuan Dynasty, and unified China. He never forgot his peasant roots; during his reign, he emphasized agrarian reconstruction, and treated harshly the rich and scholarly. He also worked to bring peace to China and rebuild its defenses.

Mausoleum of Dr. Sun Yat-sen

Dr. SUN YAT-SEN WAS one of the single most influential individuals in China's long history. As the leader of the Revolution of 1911, he deserves the lion's share of the credit for bringing the more than two thousand-year-old imperial system of government in China to an end, and replacing it with the more democratic Republic of China.

Sun Yat-sen was born on November 12, 1866, in Cuiheng Village, Xiangshan County, near the city of Canton in southern China. Xiangshan County was close to the port of Macao, hence its residents often came into contact with foreigners. At the age of twelve, Sun Yat-sen traveled to Honolulu, Hawaii, to study. He graduated from Oahu College, and returned at age seventeen to study medicine in Hong Kong. He graduated from the College of Medicine in 1892.

In addition to his medical skill, Dr. Sun had a strong interest in politics. He believed the Qing Dynasty was intolerably corrupt, and made it his mission to overthrow imperialism. He began by forming the Xing Zhong Hui (Society for the Revival of China), a group dedicated to establishing government by the people. In 1905, he united several other revolutionary groups under the name Tong Meng Hui (Revolutionary League). He debated openly with monarchists, and staged armed attempts at rebellion—meeting with continual failure for more than a decade, but never losing hope.

Finally, in 1911, a rebellion broke out in Wuchang and quickly spread to other provinces. The revolutionary forces in Wuhan held a conference at which they created a provisional government that supplanted the rule of the Qing. This successful uprising became known as the Revolution of 1911, and represented the beginning of a new era in Chinese history. Dr. Sun Yat-sen was named president of the Republic of China on New Year's Day of 1912. In the years that followed, he continued working as a political activist, trying to ensure the success of the Republic. In the autumn of 1923, he was invited to Beijing by Fen Yu-xiang, who had staged a successful coup. Two years later, still living in Beijing, Dr. Sun Yat-sen died of liver cancer.

The Mausoleum of Dr. Sun Yat-sen, called *Zhongshanling*, is located on Zijin (Purple Gold) Mountain—also known as Zhongshan Mountain in honor of Dr. Sun's revolutionary alias *Zhongshanqiao*. As early as 1912, thirteen years before his death, Dr. Sun had visited Zijin Mountain, and requested of his friends that he be buried there when he died. The mausoleum, designed by Lu Yanzhi, is in the shape of an alarm bell, signifying Dr. Sun's desire to "arouse the masses." The Sacrificial Hall is built of granite, in a symmetrical style typical of traditional Chinese architecture.

Chengde Mountain Resort and Outlying Temples

HEBEI PROVINCE

ONE OF CHINA'S best-known scenic and historic attractions, the Chengde Mountain Resort and Outlying Temples were a summer resort for the emperors of the Qing Dynasty (1644–1911). Construction of the first palaces began in 1703, during the reign of Emperor Kangxi, and continued during the reign of his grandson Qianlong, through the year 1792.

The Summer Resort, also known as Bishushanzhuang (Fleeing-the-Heat Mountain Villa) covers a total area of 5.61 square kilometers, and consists of two parts: the palace grounds, full of administrative and ceremonial buildings, and the imperial gardens that surround them. A vast landscape of lakes, pastures, and forests includes ninety pavilions, twenty-six causeways and bridges, over sixty rockeries, sixteen gardens and temples, and twenty-five inscribed steles and rock inscriptions. Seventy-two spots of particular scenic interest bear inscriptions written by one of the two emperors—thirty-six selected by Kangxi, and thirty-six by Qianlong. The landscaping combines qualities of North China's elegant simplicity, and the more ornate style of the South. The eight temples to the northeast of the Resort, too, include styles of several different nationalities.

Putuo Zhongsheng Temple, the Temple of Potaraka Doctrine (pictured at left) is a miniature version of the Potala Palace in Lhasa. It was built in 1767, the thirty-second year of Emperor Qianlong's reign, to host his sixtieth birthday celebration three years later. Chieftains from the neighboring lands of Tibet, Qinghai, Mongolia, and Xinjiang came to attend the celebration.

Dahongtai Palace, the main part of Putuo Zhongsheng Temple, stands seven stories tall, atop a mountain covered with trees. Within the palace are smaller, three-story buildings arranged around a central square. These buildings, which served as resting places for the emperor during his visits to the temple, still contain artifacts that were used in religious ceremonies, such as musical instruments and sacrificial vessels. Although the palace itself is built in a Tibetan style, the pavilions and houses visible on top–in another example of cultural blending–show the distinctive hallmarks of Han architecture.

Xumi Fushou Temple, the Temple of Happiness and Longevity (pictured at right), was built in 1780, the forty-fifth year of Qianlong's reign, to honor the sixth Panchen Lama when he came to Qianlong's seventieth birthday celebration.

The Chengde Mountain Resort was designated as a World Heritage site by UNESCO in 1987.

Potala Palace

POTALA PALACE, LOCATED 130 meters above The Lhasa valley on Red Hill, and itself standing 178 meters tall, is the world's highest palace, and is generally considered to be the greatest monumental structure in all of Tibet. It once served as the main residence of the Dalai Lama, the spiritual leader of Tibetan Buddhism.

The original palace built on the Red Hill was known as Kukhar Potrang. It was built in the seventh century by the Emperor Songtsen Gampo, for his bride, the Han nationality princess Wencheng. Although it was burned down by lightning and war, and little is known about its original form or size, it is believed that there are still two rooms that were part of the original palace within the current structure's total of one thousand rooms. The palace as it exists today was built during the seventeenth century, during the reign of the Fifth Dalai Lama. Its construction demanded the efforts of more than nine thousand workers, artists, and craftsmen. It is believed that the present name, "Potala Palace," derives from Mt. Potala, the mythological home of the Bodhisattva Chenresi in India. Emperor Songtsen Gampo, in fact, had been viewed as an incarnation of Chenresi.

Potala Palace is composed of the Red Palace and the White Palace, named for the color of their walls. The Red Palace was added to Potala between 1690 and 1694. It is used primarily for religious matters and includes shrines, stupas (reliquary monuments), an assembly hall for the monks, and the tombs of eight Dalai Lamas. The White Palace, built earlier than the Red Palace (between 1645 and 1653), is used for politics and daily living. It contains a seminary, a printing workshop, and living quarters. The entire structure stands thirteen stories tall, and has an interior space of more than 130,000 square meters.

In 1922, the Thirteenth Dalai Lama renovated many of the chapels and assembly halls in the White Palace, and added two stories to the Red Palace. In 1994, a group of skilled Tibetan architects and technicians completed an extensive renovation of the palace, without any damage or loss of relics.

The Forest of Stupas at Shaolin Temple

HENAN PROVINCE

THE CEMETERY KNOWN AS the Forest of Stupas, located 300 meters northwest of Shaolin Temple, was built during the dynasties from the Tang through the Qing. The ashes of the temple's abbots and high-ranking monks are stored in stone sculptures (stupas) of various shapes and sizes. Among the 243 stupas are rectangular shapes, cylindrical, hexagonal, conical, round, and bottle-shaped; they have from one to seven tiers, and the tallest is 15 meters high. The Forest of Stupas is considered a miniature treasury of ancient stone sculpture and architecture.

Shaolin Temple was built in A.D. 495, near the base of Mt. Songshan in Dengfeng County, Henan Province. Its founder was an Indian monk named Batuo, who received the land as a gift from Emperor Xiaowen of the Northern Wei Dynasty. The temple specialized in scholarly translation of Buddhist scripture into Chinese, but did not become truly famous until the arrival of a second Indian monk, Bodhidharma, in A.D. 527.

Bodhidharma created the Chan (Zen) sect of Buddhism, which quickly became the most widely accepted form of Buddhism in China. He also invented a series of exercises for the monks who trained under him, having found them too weak to engage in his demanding meditation practices. One of these exercises became known as "The Eighteen Hand Movements of the Enlightened One." Those eighteen movements formed the foundation of Shaolin kung fu, also known as *wushu*.

The Shaolin monks continued to develop their martial arts skills out of necessity—even hiring kung fu masters from outside the temple to train them—because the temple was frequently menaced by bandits. In time, those monks known as "Protectors of the Temple" were able to repel the bandits on their own. In the early seventh century, after thirteen martial monks saved Emperor Li Shimin of the Tang Dynasty from danger, he proclaimed Shaolin the "Number One Temple under Heaven." Since then, *Shaolin Quan Fa* (the Way of the Shaolin Fist) has enjoyed a high reputation among the martial arts.

Today, the region's primary industry is tourism, particularly by students of the martial arts. In fact, most of the "monks" a tourist will see are actors, participating in a historical recreation of what temple life once was. There are five private and one government-operated martial arts schools near the temple, with a total of more than six thousand students. Two of the most important "secrets" of Shaolin kung fu training are hard work and specialization. An old saying asserts: "I do not fear the ten thousand kicks you have practiced once. I fear the one kick you have practiced ten thousand times."

Yellow Crane Tower

HUBEI PROVINCE

YELLOW CRANE TOWER was first built in A.D. 223, during the Three Kingdoms Period. Although the precise details of why it was originally constructed have been lost to history, there is a charming legend that tells of a Taoist sage who drew a crane on the wall of a wine shop, to thank the wine merchant, a Mrs. Xin, for her gift of a thousand cups of free wine. The priest told the "magical" crane drawing to dance and bring good fortune to Mrs. Xin, and forever after the wine shop was full of customers. Ten years later, the sage returned and flew away on the crane to become an Immortal. Mrs. Xin, by then a rich woman, built the Yellow Crane Tower in his honor.

The tower is located on Yellow Crane Rock, on Snake Hill in Wuchang, on the Changjiang River's south bank. The structure was destroyed and rebuilt many times in the dynasties following its construction, including four times during the Qing Dynasty. The most recent reconstruction took place between November of 1981 and June of 1985. The present tower is larger than any of its predecessors—20 meters taller than its previous incarnation, at 51.4 meters high. With five stories (compared to the previous tower's three) and five upturned eaves, decorative paintings inside and out, and covered with yellow glaze, Yellow Crane Tower is at once majestic and refined.

The tower is part of a compound that includes side pavilions, memorial archways, corridors of inscribed tablets, and the four-storied White Cloud Tower. Together, the two towers give Wuhan its nickname "home of the yellow crane in white clouds."

Yellow Crane Tower has inspired more than a thousand poems. The best-known is "Yellow Crane Tower," by Cui Hao. Many Chinese students learn to recite this poem by heart. It reads:

The sage on a yellow crane was gone amid
*   clouds white.*
To what avail does Yellow Crane Tower remain?
Once gone, the Yellow Crane will never
*   on earth alight.*
Only white clouds still float from year to year
*   in vain.*
By a sunlit river, trees can be counted one by one;
On Parrot Island, sweet green grass grows
*   fast and thick.*
Where is my native land lit by the setting sun?
Veiled waves of Hanjiang make one homesick.

Leshan Buddha

AT 71 METERS (232 FEET) HIGH, and 28 meters wide, the Giant Buddha at Leshan is so large that two people can stand side by side in one of his ears, and as many as a hundred people can sit on each of his feet. This representation of the Buddha Maitreya is not only the largest stone statue of a Buddha anywhere in the world, it is the world's largest stone sculpture of *anything*. The seated figure is larger than the tallest Buddha at Bamian in Afghanistan, which is standing.

In ancient times, the convergence of the Minjiang, Dadu, and Qingyi rivers made the city of Leshan a major crossroads and trading center of southern Sichuan. Silk and textiles from Chengdu and the bountiful agricultural products of the Chuanxi Plains were transported down the Minjiang River to Leshan and from there down the Qingyi to the rest of China. But the turbulent currents where the three rivers met also spelled great danger for the boats that traveled these waters. In A.D. 713, a Tang Dynasty Buddhist monk named Haitong decided to create a giant statue of a Buddha to protect the passing ships. The Leshan Buddha is built into an overhanging cliff in the Xiluo Peak of Lingyun Mountain, on the eastern bank overlooking the confluence of the three rivers, with his back against Mount Jiuding, and staring across at Mount Emei on the far side. The statue was completed after Haitong's death, in A.D. 803.

Although its features have been eroded to some extent and there is foliage growing on the Buddha's body, the statue has remained surprisingly whole over the last twelve hundred years. This is due in large part to the presence of a well-designed drainage system, hidden within and under the carved figure. Some crude restoration has been carried out on the inner sides of the legs.

Mt. Emei, at which the giant Buddha stares, has historically been a site of great significance for Chinese Buddhists and is referred to as the Buddhist Paradise and the Celestial World on Earth. It is a place of pilgrimage and is also visited by artists, writers, scientists, and tourists. Both Mt. Emei and the Leshan Buddha have been designated as World Heritage Sites by UNESCO.

Xuankong (Suspended) Temple

SHANXI PROVINCE

I T IS NOT UNCOMMON ON China's scenic mountains to see oddly shaped rocks that resemble monkeys, pagodas, and the like. Nor is it uncommon to see vegetation growing on mountainsides. But on the foothills of Mount Hengshan, the northernmost of the Taoist faith's Five Sacred Mountains, an entire temple appears to have grown from the face of a cliff.

The group of Buddhist temples called Xuankong (Suspended) Monastery, known more poetically as the Mid-Air Temple, is an extraordinary sight—universally acknowledged as the foremost of the eighteen scenic spots on Mount Hengshan. It is located midway up a cliff on the western side of Cuiping Peak, near the mouth of the Jinlong River. The structure contains a total of forty rooms, divided among several buildings at higher and lower levels, connected by staircases and pathways of wooden planks. While two main buildings are resting on outcroppings of solid rock, the foundations of the other buildings consist of slim wooden posts sunk into holes in the cliff face.

Xuankong Temple is a frightening place to visit, with a precipitous valley beneath and large overhanging rocks perched above, looking as though they might fall at any moment. The plank pathways creak underfoot, and some of the supporting pillars look scarcely thicker than chopsticks. But the structure has stood since the last years of the Northern Wei Dynasty in the sixth century; it has been renovated three or four times in the intervening centuries, but has never collapsed nor suffered serious damage. Tucked into a hollow in the cliff, it is protected from the area's violent winds, and the tall peaks across the valley shield it from the sun for all but three hours a day, which has likely contributed to its endurance. While the paths between buildings are excitingly precarious, the buildings themselves are as steady as if they had been built on ground.

Although it is appealing to think that the ancient architects might have constructed the Suspended Temple just to prove that it was possible, there were also practical considerations behind that decision. The Hunhe River running through the valley made it an important route for travel and communication in ancient times, and therefore a natural and convenient place to situate a temple. However, the river flooded with every storm, and might have washed away a ground-based temple— so the architects devised a way to build it at a safer elevation.

Qiyuan Temple on Jiuhua Mountain

FROM THE AZURE SKIES *above descends a jade-like flow,*
And nine fascinating lotuses rise out of the hills below.

The poet Li Bai penned those lines while observing Jiuzi Mountain from a riverbank at its base, seeing in its crests the shape of nine lotus blossoms. It was from this poem that the mountain acquired its present name, Jiuhua (Nine Lotuses). Today, Jiuhua is one of the four most important Buddhist mountains in China, along with Mt. Emei (in Sichuan Province), Mt. Wutai (in Shanxi Province), and Mt. Putuo (in Zhejiang Province).

Located in Qingyang County of Anhui Province, Jiuhuashan is known as the most picturesque mountain in China's southeast. In an area of 100 square kilometers, there are a total of ninety-nine peaks, the tallest of which, Shiwang Peak, towers 1,340 meters high. Its daunting crags are covered with evergreen trees, and its peaks are interspersed with waterfalls and streams, fountains and tranquil pools. Over the years, people have seen many interesting shapes in the mountain's rocks, and named them. There is a stone shaped like a roc listening to a sermon, Wooden Fish Stone, and Buddha's Belly in Sunshine, to name a few.

Buddhism first came to Jiuhuashan in the Northern and Southern Dynasties (A.D. 420–581). Monks lived in the mountain's many caves, or, like the monk Fuhu in A.D. 503, built small convents. In the year 713, a Korean Buddhist named Jin Qiaojue came to the mountain to live in a cave. On his death several decades later, it was said that the Earth shook and animals wept. Jin Qiaojue came to be revered posthumously as the Earth Buddha, and the mountain became a center for rites worshiping the God of Earth. In its heyday, the mountain hosted 150 temples, and more than three thousand monks and nuns. More than fifty temples remain, well-preserved, along with some six thousand Buddha sculptures and other relics.

Qiyuan Temple, pictured here, is one of the four largest Buddhist temples on the mountain. It was built during the reign of the Ming Dynasty Emperor Jiajing (1522–1566), and underwent several renovations during the Qing Dynasty (1644–1911). The temple was named for the garden of Qiyuan, where, according to legend, Sakyamuni (the founder of Buddhism) preached for more than twenty years.

Diamond Throne Stupa

THE CITY OF HOHHOT, situated on the Huanghe (Yellow) River, is the capital of the Inner Mongolia Autonomous Region. It appears as a large raised oasis in the middle of a grassland desert known as the Tumuochuan Plain, and derives its name from that fact —*Hohhot* means "green city" in Mongolian. According to local legend, the city was built over four hundred years ago by a clan of Mongols whose leader was a direct descendant of Genghis Khan. The late Qing Dynasty Empress Dowager Ci Xi grew up in Hohhot.

One of the more interesting sights in Hohhot is the Wuta (Five Pagoda) Temple, located on a street of the same name. The main structure in this temple is a monument known as the Diamond Throne Stupa. Constructed in the year 1727, during the reign of Emperor Yongzheng of the Qing Dynasty, this stupa consists of five pagodas—each six meters tall—arranged on a square base seven meters in height. The base is known as the "Diamond Throne." The central pagoda is seven stories high, and those on the corners of the base are each five stories. The entire structure is made of glazed bricks and stone, and is decorated all over with carvings of Buddhist icons, scriptures, and floral designs. The Five Pagoda Temple belongs to the Lamaist sect of Buddhism, which is the traditional religion of Hohhot.

The construction of Buddhist temples in China flourished after the first century, and pagodas—originally an Indian concept—came to China during the reign of Sun Quan (229–252) of the State of Wu, according to historical records. Though there remains no trace of the first pagoda, it is estimated that China now contains some two thousand pagodas. A pagoda tends to resemble a stack of overturned bowls, with an odd number of stories and an even number of sides—usually square, hexagonal, or octagonal. They can be built of wood, stone, brick, tile, iron, or bronze, and appear singly, or in groups of over a hundred.

Hohhot's Wuta Temple has a predecessor in the Haidian District of Beijing. Zhenjue Temple, the Temple of True Awakening, built in the year 1473 during the Ming Dynasty, also consists of five pagodas on a square "Diamond Throne" base. Originally conceived as an imitation of Baddha Gaya in central India, Zhenjue Temple nonetheless incorporates some stylistic elements native to China.

The Three Pagodas of Saintly Worship

IT HAS BEEN SAID THAT the Tang Dynasty is noted for its temples and the Song Dynasty for its pagodas, but the pagodas of the Tang Dynasty, though not as numerous as those of the Song, have a distinctive architectural style of their own. In addition to the well-known Lesser Wild Goose Pagoda in the ancient imperial capital of Xi'an, the Three Pagodas of Chongsheng Temple near the city of Dali, Yunnan Province, are excellent examples of that style.

The *Miyan* (close-eaved) style of pagoda tends to have relatively short upper stories on top of a taller ground level, such that the upper eaves are spaced close together. The interiors of these pagodas are usually cramped and dark, and windows, if they are present at all, are small. The elegant simplicity of this style is best appreciated from a distance, so that the pagoda may be viewed as a single, unified whole.

The Three Pagodas of Saintly Worship (Chongsheng Santa), among the oldest extant structures in southwestern China, are the remnants of the ancient Chongsheng Monastery. The once-prosperous temple now lies in ruins at the feet of the pagodas, damaged by earthquakes, but the pagodas have withstood the elements admirably over the centuries. The tallest of the three, a sixteen-tiered structure named Qianxun Pagoda, was built between the years of 836 and 876, and stands 69.13 meters high. The other two, to its west and north, are ten-tiered pagodas each 42.19 meters tall, and were built later, during the tenth century. All three are narrow-looking octagonal spires, made of bricks painted white. Located at the foot of Cangshan Mountain, with their reflections visible in the water of nearby Erhai Lake, the pagodas look all the more striking.

Chongsheng Monastery was a Buddhist temple, as evidenced by the carved shrines with Buddhist statues and lotus flowers found in each pagoda. During the 1978 reconstruction, more than six hundred relics from the seventh- through tenth-century states of Dali and Nanzhao were discovered. These items are now on display in an adjoining museum.

The pagodas were built for two main purposes. First, they served as storage places for scriptures and holy relics, and for the ashes and skeletal remains of saints. Second, an inscription on the front of Qianxun Pagoda reads "Subdue Forever the Mountains and Rivers," indicating that the temple called upon Buddha to protect the region from natural disasters such as earthquakes and floods.

Flying Dragon White Pagoda

THE SOUTHERNMOST DISTRICT of Yunnan Province, where China shares a border with Laos, Myanmar, and Vietnam, is an exciting region known as the Xishuangbanna Dai Autonomous Prefecture. Roughly 17 percent of Xishuangbanna's land area is taken up by scenic resorts and nature reserves. The climate there is subtropical, and the region is nicknamed "Aerial Garden" for its rain forests, monsoon jungles, and incredible variety of plant and animal life. The animal life includes wild Asian elephants and oxen, peacocks, hornbills, and red-necked cranes, lorises, and gibbons. Among the more extraordinary plants are the eight hundred-year-old "King of Tea Trees," and the "color-changing flower," which changes colors, chameleon-like, three times a day.

The city of Jinghong, located just over 700 kilometers from the provincial capital of Kunming, is the district capital of Xishuangbanna. The Dai nationality people who are native to Jinghong are primarily Buddhists, and the most impressive sights in the city are the temples, pagodas, and pavilions built to honor that faith. Many thousands of Buddhists travel to Jinghong to worship at these sites every year.

The White Pagoda, pictured here, sits on a hill behind Manfeilong village, in the neighborhood of Damenglong town. Built in the year 1204, it is also known as "Bamboo Pagoda," for its resemblance to a bundle of bamboo shoots. The central tower is an elaborately shaped spike 16.29 meters tall, and it is surrounded by eight smaller pagodas, at the outer edge of a pedestal 8.6 meters in diameter. The surface of the White Pagoda is decorated with carvings of Buddhas, flowers, and animals. Nearby in Damenglong is this structure's brother, the Black Pagoda.

A few of the other significant Buddhist sites in the city include Manting Temple and the Octagonal Pavilion. Located in the middle of Manting Park, Manting Temple was the first Buddhist temple built in Xishuangbanna. It has stood since the year 615, and even today, it is the most important temple in the region. The Octagonal Pavilion is located at Jingzhen, in Mengzhe township. Constructed in 1701, the pavilion is said to have been built in the shape of the golden headgear of Sakyamuni, the founder of Buddhism. Small bronze bells hang from the eaves of the pavilion, and they chime with the breezes.

For information about Hugh Lauter Levin Associates
publications, please refer to our web site, at:

http://www.HLLA.com